Praise for *Hap*

"Roni Habib is a student whisperer who writes with breathtaking clarity about how to unlock human potential in the classroom. Through his generous, thoughtful, and practical manual on pedagogy, you'll learn to engage *all* students, particularly the most vulnerable. A must-read for any educator, mentor, coach, or parent. It'll even help you better understand yourself!"

—**Julie Lythcott-Haims,** *New York Times* bestselling author of *How to Raise an Adult*

"This unique collection of practical strategies for building a positive and inclusive classroom environment will serve as an indispensable guide for new and veteran teachers alike. As educators, we know the importance of developing practices that foster connections with our students. This book creates a road map that will make you laugh, reflect, think, and, most importantly, grow as a person on this professional journey."

—**Marianne Chowning-Dray**, Recipient of Presidential Award for Excellence in Mathematics and Science Teaching from President Barack Obama

"As a veteran superintendent, I have seen firsthand the transformative impact that Roni Habib and his company EQ Schools have had on educators across the country. In this groundbreaking book, Roni shares his expertise on the power of positivity, emotional intelligence, and mindfulness, and how these skills can help educators not only find happiness and peace but also become more effective at reaching and inspiring their students. Through practical tips, engaging activities, and real-life stories from classrooms, this book provides a road map for creating and sustaining joyful, connected, and effective learning environments. Whether you're a new teacher or a seasoned educator, the insights and strategies in this book will help you thrive both in and outside the classroom. I highly recommend this book to anyone who wants to unlock their full potential as an educator and make a lasting impact on the lives of their students."

—**Terry Walker**, Superintendent of Irvine Unified School District

Happy & Resilient

HAPPY & RESILIENT

The Complete Guide to Joyful Teaching, Learning, and Living

RONI HABIB

Happy & Resilient: The Complete Guide to Joyful Teaching, Learning, and Living
© 2023 Roni Habib

This book is available at special discounts when purchased in quantity for educational purposes or for use as premiums, promotions, or fundraisers. For inquiries and details, contact the publisher at books@daveburgessconsulting.com.

Published by Dave Burgess Consulting, Inc.
San Diego, CA
DaveBurgessConsulting.com

Library of Congress Control Number: 2023947653
Paperback ISBN: 978-1-956306-57-6
Ebook ISBN: 978-1-956306-58-3

Cover and interior design by Liz Schreiter
Edited and produced by Reading List Editorial
ReadingListEditorial.com

To my ima ve aba (mother and father), Simona and Isaac Habib, for modeling what living joyfully and resiliently looks like, for your everlasting belief in me, and for your beautiful and unconditional love.

CONTENTS

INTRODUCTION

*I learned a lot from my teachers,
more from my friends, and the
most from my students.*

—Rabbi Chanina

Inor Bibah

It was the middle of April in my third year of teaching, and it was my first year teaching AP Economics at one of the highest-performing, highest-pressure high schools in the nation. I was nervous about doing a good job and determined to help my students both earn college credit and learn to apply economics to real life. I was about to teach them a concept that is difficult even for grad students to fully understand, and I was not going to mess it up. I had spent a week preparing for this lesson, thinking carefully about how to introduce the concept meaningfully with a great hook, about the scaffolding I would need to provide, the formative assessments I would embed, and even what specific words I would use in my direct instruction.

As soon as the bell rang, I was all business. I took roll quickly and immediately delved into my hook, which was followed by my meticulously crafted lecture. The classroom was completely silent except for my voice. The students were taking copious notes, and their body language and facial expressions suggested that they were fully with me. It felt good to be so prepared and to feel like such an amazing teacher. I knew that I had them.

Until all of a sudden, Aylon Steinhart, a genius of a student who always had an odd way of thinking about things, started snickering to himself loudly enough to draw attention. I ignored it, hoping he was not going to disrupt the momentum I'd established for this lesson. I could tell that he was trying to contain himself, but he couldn't, and the snickers turned to full-on laughter. For the life of me, I couldn't understand what was so funny.

At that point, I used my proximity trick of getting close to him without saying anything that would distract from the lesson. That only made the laughter intensify, and when I stared at him, he said (in between giggles), "I'm sorry, I'm sorry," trying to compose himself.

Other students started to giggle.

I paused my lesson and told the class to take a deep breath and get refocused. I went back to the front of the class, ready to resume the lesson. I gave Aylon one last look, hoping to see that he was fully composed and ready to learn. Instead he busted out laughing uncontrollably.

"Mind sharing with us what's so funny?" I asked.

He replied, "I'm sorry, I'm sorry, don't worry about it."

By this time I was really curious. "Sure you don't want to bring us in on it?"

"OK, but please don't be mad at me. I just realized that your name spelled backward is Inor Bibah!"

Half a second after he said that, the entire class, including myself, started laughing out loud, uncontrollably, for a good fifteen seconds. When we'd calmed down a bit, I asked him, still giggling a little, "So over the last five minutes you were working on spelling my name backward instead of paying attention to my lecture?" For some reason that realization was super funny to me, and I started laughing again, with my students following me. After another twenty seconds, we all calmed down. I could feel how much more relaxed and joyful my students were from laughing together and eventually (after a few more deep breaths) learning together.

This taught me that no matter how important, technical, or difficult a concept is, there is always room for laughter and connection, and laughter actually brings a group together in a way that is truly special. A joyful, fun, and inclusive climate that fosters laughter is ideal for creativity and deep learning. Years later, I discovered that Daniel Goleman had coined a term for what happened in my classroom: *emotional resonance*. ER occurs when our limbic system, the emotion-processing part of the brain, is in sync in a positive way with other people's limbic systems. It is a key determinant in effective leadership, effective teaching, and group performance.

I also learned not to take myself so seriously. I could have spent a month preparing for this lesson and Aylon's brain would have still been working on spelling my name backward instead of listening to me. Stepping out of the lesson, taking time to get curious about Aylon's experience, and then laughing with my students brought us closer together, and ironically it was what led to the lesson flowing beautifully after that.

I realized that because I cannot control what my students are thinking, it pays to take some time to connect with them on a human level first. Doing this raises the likelihood that they will engage with my teaching. Yes, preparing well for lessons is important, having clear objectives is important, scaffolding is important, formative assessment is important. That said, in the practice of teaching (not just the theory of teaching), it's essential that a teacher also take time to connect with students on a human level. This is the ingredient that allows all the other elements of instruction to flow well. It is critical for students' well-being *and* for teachers' well-being.

I started consciously incorporating more community building, but I worried that I might not be serving my students academically. However, Aylon and his peers ended up doing very well on the AP test, and some even decided to major in economics. When I would run into them years later, they would tell me how much they'd liked my class. They rarely remembered the economic concepts, but they remembered how they felt. That convinced me of the importance of making a classroom climate joyful, psychologically safe, and emotionally intelligent. Today Aylon is in his early thirties, and he's the CEO of a successful vegan ice cream company that is growing rapidly. He seems very happy. And yes, he still calls me Inor every time we reconnect.

> *I've learned that people will forget what you said, people will forget what you did, but people will never forget how you made them feel.*
>
> —Maya Angelou

The book you are holding in your hands contains practical ideas, skills, and practices that will support your teaching in the classroom, your leadership at school, and your well-being and resilience. You can think of it as a manual to get better results in the classroom as well as a pragmatic, research-based personal development book. At the time of writing this book, I've taught and worked with students and teachers for two decades. I've had the privilege of teaching and training thousands of educators in over one hundred schools in the US as well as educators in South Korea, India, Kazakhstan, and Europe.

My journey has crystallized an important truth: educators who are happier and more resilient are much better educators. This is because happier people, in general, have a performance advantage over others, but it's also because teaching is a deeply relational endeavor at its core, and we cannot be emotionally (or intellectually) available to others unless we are first emotionally available to ourselves. Besides medicine, I cannot think of a profession that involves as much trust as teaching. Students are deeply reliant on us, not only for academic support but for emotional support as well. And that is true for all ages, preschool to college. Investing in our well-being, resilience, and presence allows us to thrive, but it also allows us to be the kind of educators that students can rely on, the kind that can help them thrive as well.

After scouring the scientific literature for many years, investigating the fields of positive psychology, interpersonal neurobiology, organizational development, education, applied mindfulness, emotional intelligence, and more, I took the most powerful, researched-based ideas and applied them to the reality we face as educators and as human beings. A few of the ideas in this book are my originals, but most are borrowed from much smarter people.

How to Read This Book

I'm not here to tell you how to teach. I know that you already know how to teach. I'm here to give you suggestions. Take as many as you want. You are a leader of people, and no matter how young or old they are, the better you feel, the more they are going to benefit. So you can use this book as a guide for your growth and well-being, as a guide for effective teaching, or you can use it for both. My biggest hope is that you, dear educator, will put some of the ideas laid out in this book into practice to improve your own life. If you do, you will likely see powerful, long-lasting results, and this will naturally lead you to become an even more effective educator than you already are.

Educators are busy, so I purposely structured this book so that you can read it from start to finish or skip around to find what is most valuable to you. That said, I believe you'll get the most out of reading it all, and I recommend you read chapter 1 because it provides a road map for the book.

Every chapter will give you a set of skills to help you thrive as an educator and as a person. The book also includes practical activities to use in the classroom with students or at school with your staff, journal prompts to deepen your reflection, and graphic organizers that recap the core exercises. These are the exercises that you want to stick to over time to see consistent, powerful results.

Disclaimer

Most of the practices, skills, activities, and exercises in the book are research based and have proved to help countless people, educators, and students for decades. While I feel confident that you will benefit as well, you should know that I'm not a mental health professional. The content of this book is for informational purposes only and is not intended as a substitute for professional advice, diagnosis, or treatment.

ONE

GETTING ON THE RAAMP TO THRIVING

Happiness should be taught as a skill in schools, for it is through understanding how to create our own happiness that we truly unlock our potential.

—Matthieu Ricard

My teaching journey started at Fenway High School in inner city Boston (I could see Fenway Park's scoreboard from my classroom!). I knew right away that I was meant to teach: I loved my students, their aha moments of insight, and the gift of helping them to believe in themselves. After two years of freezing in Boston, I decided to move back to California and teach at the high school I had attended as a student. I loved my first few years of teaching there, but by my fourth year, I was burning out. I was exhausted by the amount of work and started losing touch with why I became a teacher in the first place. I even considered quitting at the end of the year, but I had an intense wake-up call that spring.

One morning, I parked my car and walked toward my classroom. Before I could get to it, the intercom announced an emergency staff meeting. I entered the choir room and sat down with all my colleagues, waiting to hear the news. A couple of minutes later, our principal came in looking completely distraught. She told us that one of our students had died by suicide. She announced his name. He was my student. That moment broke me.

Because he had died in a public way, jumping in front of a train, the news was about to break, so we had to be ready to support our students. At the end of that devastating day, I got an email from his mother. She wrote that her son had a real connection with me because he enjoyed my class and loved the camp I ran for students interested in social justice. She asked me to speak at his funeral, and while it would be the hardest thing I'd ever had to do, I wanted to honor him and support the family, so of course I said yes.

That Saturday I got to the church and sat in the first row with my student's family and some of my other students. I heard the mother speak about her child. I heard the dad speak about his child. And then it was my turn to go up and speak. I quickly pulled myself together and delivered my speech. I don't know if this has ever happened to you, and what I'm about to say may make me sound like a tree-hugging hippie, but at the end of my speech, I felt a massive force channel through me. It led me to make a vow: as long as I continued to be an educator, *nothing* was going to stop me from putting my students' well-being first. Nothing. No matter what subject I was teaching them, I was going to teach them how to be well first. The only problem was that I wasn't well. I was still burned out and now also traumatized. I was far from feeling well. And since kids can smell bullshit from a mile away, if I was going to teach them how to be well, I had to start with myself.

I saw a therapist, started using mindfulness practices, started working out regularly, and utilized positive psychology principles that completely transformed my mindset and heartset. Within three months I had more energy, I had reconnected to my passion for teaching, I was excited to go to work, I was way more creative, and my students thought I was on drugs (I promised I wasn't). I decided that if I had these skills as an adult, I could teach them to students, and I created an elective class called Positive Psychology. I was praying that twenty-five students would sign up, otherwise the class wouldn't be able to run. When 107 students signed up, I was blown away.

The message was clear: kids want to know how to be well. I taught sixteen sections of this course for four years and saw hundreds of students behaviorally shift in front of my eyes. It was so powerful that I started using some of the strategies from Positive Psych in my AP Econ and history classes, and the results were even better than I'd hoped. Students learned more, felt more connected, were happier, and were more resilient. I decided to create workshops for other educators on how to embed these strategies into their classrooms and their lives. The impact on the well-being and performance of these educators and their students was immediate and powerful. As the workshops mushroomed into summits and conferences, I founded EQ Schools, and in addition to supporting educators in the classroom, I started supporting administrators and parents to help schools and districts create a climate that is joyful, emotionally intelligent, equitable, and safe—a climate where students and adults can thrive.

I often start my workshops with a powerful visualization that I invite you to do with me now. In a moment you will close your eyes and visualize the face of a child that you love. This can be a student of yours, it can be a niece or a nephew, or it can be your own child. If you have multiple kids, choose your favorite. I know, I know, it's hard to pick, but see if you can really just choose one child. Got it? I'd like you to imagine that this child is smiling at you, and I want you to visualize their face with as many details as you can. For example, do they have a dimple in their cheek? Is there a twinkle in their eye? What happens to their eyebrows as they smile? Spend one minute visualizing this child smiling at you and allow yourself to be filled up with joy from that experience.

After a minute, ask yourself the following question and notice the first word that comes to mind. (Don't think about it for long at all—just see what comes up naturally.) The question is this: What do you most want this child to have in their life? Notice the first word that comes up, and jot it down.

If I had to bet on it, I would say that the first word you thought of was *happiness* or something like it, such as *peace, contentment, love,* etc. I say this because I do this visualization with thousands of people every year, and no matter what culture they belong to or where in the world I am speaking, the vast majority say *happiness.* As adults, that's what we care about the most for our children, what we want the most for them. It's amazing to me how prevalent and consistent that answer is across the board. By the way, if you didn't say *happiness,* you are still a wonderful person.

When I delve deeper with my participants to find out what's behind their answer, they realize what they really want is for their children to optimize their well-being. Happiness occurs when we experience positive emotions, and this is usually a momentary experience. Well-being consists of feeling good and functioning well. It's having the experience of positive emotions from time to time as well as developing our potential, having a sense of control over our life, having a sense of purpose, and surrounding ourselves with healthy relationships. It is a sustainable condition that allows us to thrive.[1]

Yet when it comes to school, well-being gets shoved aside because of our notion of what school should be. School is for academics, for rigor, for the development of the intellect, and for giving students skills that will make them productive members of our society. Don't get me wrong—all these things are incredibly important, and it's wonderful that schools provide these to students. Yet if well-being is what we care about the most, and if children spend most of their waking hours in school, why have we decided that well-being shouldn't be a focus in schools?

One reason well-being isn't prioritized in schools (beyond our mindless and unexamined view of what school should be) is we falsely believe that well-being is not something we have a lot of control over. You are either predisposed to it or you aren't.

Well-being doesn't just happen to us. In fact, people's well-being is determined much more by the way they interpret the events in their lives (in other words, by their explanatory style) than by the events themselves.

In the 1970s psychologists studied people who had just won the lottery and people who'd had an accident that rendered them quadriplegic.[2] While both events had a short-term impact on peoples' well-being, the research showed that in a relatively brief time, these people returned to their baseline level of happiness (BLH) and neither group appeared to be happier than the other. Ironically, this research study led some psychologists to believe that our BLH is predetermined and there is nothing we can do about it. This was the prevailing belief until two decades ago.

At the beginning of this century, scientists found that while 60 percent of our happiness "pie" is determined by our neurobiology, our genes, and our environment, 40 percent of it is determined by our actions, thoughts, and attitudes.[3]

This book contains what I believe to be the most effective and most rigorously studied practices that lead us to develop the types of thoughts, attitudes, and actions that allow us to thrive in life *and* to be top educators no matter what subject or grade level we teach.

Another reason well-being is not prioritized in schools is that we erroneously believe that well-being skills cannot be taught.

Well-being and resilience, just like mathematics, can be taught. The field of positive psychology and the study of emotional intelligence have shown us that happiness and resilience skills are easily teachable, and when practiced consistently, they are highly effective at improving the quality of our life and the impact we have on others. Furthermore, activities from these fields make teaching easier, more meaningful, and more fun. It turns out that to climb from one level of well-being, resilience, and performance to another, we just need a RAAMP.

Well-being
and resilience,
just like
mathematics,
can be taught.

Introducing RAAMP

The acronym RAAMP contains the five ingredients that, according to positive psychology researchers, contribute the most to anyone's well-being. The five ingredients are:

R

Relationships
Surrounding ourselves with healthy relationships is the number one predictor of well-being and longevity.

A

Awareness
Being present so you can live life fully in the here and now without being lost in mental ruminations.

A

Advancement
Continuing to grow and pursuing goals that are personally meaningful to us.

M

Meaning
Being connected to our purpose, reason for being, and reason for engaging in our profession.

P

Positive Emotions
Experiencing at least a three-to-one ratio of positive emotions to difficult emotions in life and at work.

These ingredients are not only top predictors of well-being, but they are also a lot more predictive of a person's long-term success than any academic measure.[4] The main reason these five ingredients are the backbone of this book goes beyond well-being. It is because in my fifteen years of experience coaching and developing teachers, I've found that intentionally growing these five ingredients amplifies teachers' effectiveness in the classroom more than any other kind of professional development does. We'll take a deep dive into the skills that support each of these ingredients in the chapters ahead.

One of the simplest yet most powerful ways to understand why the elements of RAAMP are so critical to our well-being involves listening to dying people's biggest regrets.[5] I know, it's a bit heavy to remind you of death right at the beginning of this book, and I assure you that the rest of the book is lighter. But no matter how old you are, it's important to remember that you have been given the gift of being alive. And this gift is finite. Make the best of it while you are healthy enough to enjoy it.

Below are the top five regrets of the dying as observed by Bronnie Ware, an Australian nurse who spent years working in palliative care helping people in the last twelve weeks of their lives. Ware recognized that people at the end of their lives have tremendous clarity about what truly matters to them and that we could all learn from that wisdom.

Here are the top five regrets of the dying.

1. I wish I'd had the courage to live a life true to myself, not the life others expected of me.

This is the most common of the regrets. People get to the end of their lives and realize they didn't fulfill half of their dreams because they lived life on autopilot, thinking they would be healthy forever. They realize at the end that not making the choice to fulfill dreams is a choice in itself.

2. I wish I hadn't worked so hard.

Every male patient that Ware cared for shared this regret with her. They said they wished they'd spent more quality time with their children and partners.

3. I wish I'd had the courage to express my feelings.

Many people suppress their emotions and don't share how they truly feel about important parts of their lives. They decide to settle to appease others, which leads them to feel resentment later on.

4. I wish I had stayed in touch with my friends.

People underestimate the benefits true friendships provide. They get caught up in their day to day, lose touch with great friends, and end up not only missing them at the end of their lives but also regretting missing past opportunities to spend meaningful time with them.

5. I wish that I had let myself be happier.

At the end of life, people realize with great clarity that well-being truly is a choice. It's easy to get stuck in old patterns and habits and to believe that we are perfectly content when deep inside there is a longing for more laughter, joy, and positive emotions. The dying recognize that they could have experienced more of those in their lives if they'd been a little more intentional.

I bring these regrets up because when you live life more deliberately and intentionally invest in each ingredient of RAAMP, you will be a lot less likely to have these regrets at the end of your journey. Rather, you'll look back at your memories and have peace of mind, joy in your heart, and a smile on your face knowing that you made the best out of life. (R) Investing in relationships that fill your cup and using helpful communication tools, (A) being more self-aware, (A) knowing how you want to grow, (M) and what brings you meaning, and (P) intentionally infusing yourself with positive emotions through positive experiences and practices, helps to avoid these five regrets.

You'll see that as you focus on these ingredients, your students will naturally want to learn from you more. This is because you'll be more attuned to their energy and more aware of their needs and your needs. Getting more in touch with your passion for life and for teaching will magnetize your students toward you. You will collectively experience more positive interactions and emotions together, and this will strengthen your lessons and lead to more intellectual rigor that will feel joyful. Most importantly, you will be modeling and teaching skills that will help your students thrive not only in the classroom but in life.

While it may sound daunting to intentionally incorporate these ingredients into your life and your work, delve in with me. You'll see in the following chapters that RAAMPing up to thrive is easier than you may think.

TWO

RELATIONSHIPS

THERE IS NOTHING MORE IMPORTANT IN LEARNING AND LIFE

People don't care how much you know until they know how much you care.

—Theodore Roosevelt

We are social creatures that are hardwired to need to feel that we belong. That's why having supportive relationships in our lives is the number one predictor of well-being. When that need is fully met, it's easier for us to relax into whatever life throws our way.

From Rapport to Results: The Impact of Relationships on Student Academic Growth

If you have taught more than five minutes, you know that students bring their own unique set of challenges and strengths with them, just as all humans do. They can annoy, question, ignore, frustrate, anger, and upset you, other students, and themselves. But they can also cooperate, complement, collaborate, listen well, push themselves intellectually, soothe, support, and work well with you, other students, and themselves. What leads them to choose one path versus another?

There are several factors, but perhaps the most crucial is knowing that you (the adult in the room) care about them, that you see them, and that you will not give up on them. In addition, if you give them reasons to like you (to be clear, you don't need to become their friend), students will go above and beyond to learn from you and work with you and others.

Some teachers believe that whether students like them or not should have no bearing on how much or how well they learn. While that is an interesting philosophical idea to ponder, it is not rooted in an understanding of human behavior. Humans work well with humans they like and get along with. We thrive when we feel liked and when we like those around us. This is particularly crucial when it comes to learning.

Abraham Maslow proposed that once our physiological and safety needs are met, we then need to feel that we are loved and we belong.[1] Once that condition is met, we can fully engage the other parts of our brain to develop our cognitive skills and intellectual abilities. In other words, we cannot remember facts, describe new concepts, apply ideas, analyze information, evaluate points of view, or create new original work without first feeling that we belong and we are psychologically safe. That's why some educators say, "You need to Maslow before you can Bloom," referring to psychologist Benjamin Bloom's taxonomy—a hierarchical ordering of cognitive skills that many educators use to assess students' understanding.[2] These educators understand that for students to fully engage in the class and to feel safe taking intellectual risks, they need to feel seen and respected for who they are, their abilities, and what they contribute.

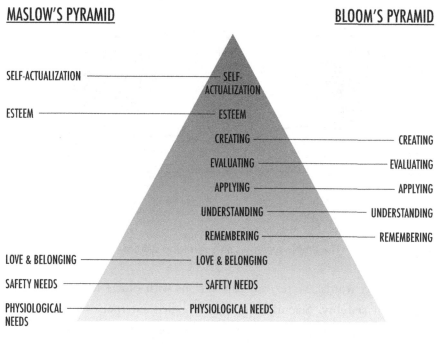

Maslow's Pyramid on left, Bloom's Pyramid on the right,
and combo pyramid in the middle.

By using effective communication tools and intentionally incorporating connection rituals, improv games, gratitude circles, and other activities, we can infuse our classrooms with emotional resonance. We feel in sync with others and it feels good to us. It's a primal experience that tells us "this person cares about my well-being, they are fun to learn with and from, it's safe for me to just be myself, and it's also safe for me to push myself to learn and grow with their support."

It's important that we provide students with skills that help them self-regulate, but it's crucial that we also understand the following: while many parts of our brain are considered self-regulating closed-loop systems, the limbic system, where we process emotions, is actually an open-loop system—meaning that it depends largely on external sources to manage itself.[3]

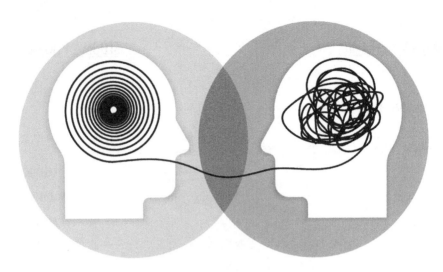

The limbic system is an open-loop system.

In other words, we rely on connections with others for our own emotional stability. Scientifically, this is called interpersonal limbic regulation, or co-regulation, and it occurs when one person transmits signals that can alter hormone levels, cardiovascular function, sleep rhythms, and even immune function inside the body of another through mirror neurons.

When we have enough awareness to recognize that our students are dysregulated, we can use powerful communication strategies to help regulate their limbic systems. Mirror neurons transmit signals in nanoseconds, which is why emotions are so contagious. We've all experienced a classroom in which students seem content and at peace until a student who is "too cool for school" shows up and begins to sour the mood of the class. It takes about five seconds before other kids begin to lose focus and start to moan and complain.

But it turns out that positive emotions are even more contagious than negative emotions.[4] They flow through us, person to person, faster. A study at Yale University showed that in groups, warmth and glee, and specifically laughter, spread most easily. The study found that these emotions had a direct influence on creativity, collaboration, and learning.

As Daniel Goleman states in his book *Primal Leadership*, "In a neurological sense, laughing represents the shortest distance between two people because it instantly interlocks limbic systems. This immediate, involuntary reaction, as one researcher puts it, involves 'the most direct communication possible between people—brain to brain—with our intellect just going along for the ride, in what might be called a 'limbic lock.'"[5]

When we hear laughter, we automatically smile or laugh, too, creating a spontaneous chain reaction that sweeps through a group. This positive hijacking boosts the academic and intellectual potential of everyone in the classroom because positive emotions flood our brains with dopamine and serotonin. These chemicals help us organize information, retain information longer, and fetch the information faster later on.

In his book *The Happiness Advantage*, Shawn Achor writes that positive emotions "enable us to make and sustain more neural connections, which allows us to think more quickly and creatively, become more skilled at complex analysis and problem solving, and see and invent new ways of doing things."[6]

Knowing this, I decided that before starting any major assessment, I would ask if anyone had a joke to share. Students loved this because whether the joke was funny or not, we always end up laughing together. This lowered their stress levels, and we would start the assessment on a higher note.

When students laugh together, have fun together, and most importantly feel psychologically safe together, they are much more likely to learn how to add fractions, how to conjugate verbs, or how cell structure works. When we infuse our classroom with positive emotions, we prime our students' brains for learning.

Relational Skills Create an Equitable Classroom Environment

I remember feeling nervous when I gave my AP Econ students their first exam, as I wasn't sure I had prepared them well for it. Yet after grading the tests, I found that about 60 percent of my students earned an A, 28 percent got a B, 6 percent got a D, and 6 percent failed the test. I was very pleased! After all, almost 90 percent of the class earned an A or a B. The same exact result replicated itself on the second test, which boosted my confidence even more. I hate to admit this (as I still feel a pang of shame to this day), but I started telling myself that I was a naturally gifted teacher. This was what I was meant to do, and these students were lucky enough to drink from the fountain of my wisdom. Wow . . . The third test showed a similar result, and while I was generally happy with this, I found the consistency of the data a bit disconcerting.

When the first report cards came out, I decided to look at how my students had fared in their other classes. Sure enough, the students who did well in my class did well in *all* their classes. These kids were gifted students who took very challenging classes and succeeded at an impressive rate. And the students who were struggling in my class? You guessed it, they struggled in almost all their classes. In other words, my colleagues and I were serving strong students really well but clearly weren't serving those who struggled on the margin.

I knew there were many reasons why students might struggle in school, but when I was presented with an opportunity to teach a Focus on Success class, which is similar to an AVID class, I began to understand more deeply what was at play. First, you should know that before teaching FOS, I thought I knew what teaching was about. I didn't. You see, the students in my FOS class pushed my buttons and challenged me in ways I'd never been challenged before. Their insecurities about school were projected onto me, and forming a strong and psychologically safe bond with them was harder. And sure, these students had learning disabilities, were academically behind, and had more social and emotional struggles than most kids. That said, many of these students were genuine geniuses when it came to things they cared about. What became clear as day to me was that the primary reason these students were struggling in school was that they doubted their ability to succeed *and* they didn't feel anyone truly cared. They felt alone and like they didn't belong in school. They got the subconscious message (rightfully or not) that they were misfits in one way or another.

I decided to ensure two things: First, each student in that class would know that I cared deeply about them and believed in their ability to succeed in school. Second, they would feel welcomed and that they belonged. I would explicitly tell them, "I believe in you, I won't give up on you, I'm here for support, and if I can't help, we'll get you someone who can. And by the way, I'm going to check in on you again tomorrow."

I checked in with each of them every day on an academic level but also a personal one. I didn't force them to share anything they didn't want to, but I gave them the opportunity to be seen and understood. I intentionally incorporated improv games into my lessons to elicit positive emotions in the class before we got to work. This enabled students to more easily talk to each other, and it made them more likely to share if they didn't understand something. I built in time for students to share how they were doing each day, which taught them listening skills. I made sure they understood that I was not pitying them, but rather that I believed in them, cared about them, and would continue to be available for them when they were ready to do the work.

Over time, and usually more slowly than I wished, they did start to feel that they belonged, and their academic achievements improved. I realized that the kids who struggled in my AP Econ class were struggling for much the same reason. They didn't feel that they belonged, so they began to give up. I decided to apply this new approach to my AP and advanced classes, and over time I saw some dramatic results. The students who'd been doing well in my classes actually did slightly better and enjoyed learning a lot more. But perhaps the most powerful part was that the previously marginalized students would now ask for help, contribute to the discussion in class, ask for feedback, come to my office hours, and be motivated to succeed because they knew that I believed in them and that they were not alone. Other students actually checked in on them, which led to new friendships and more academic rigor.

These students did not ace my class, and most of them still scored lower than the other students, but they improved their grades significantly, earning Cs and Bs. More importantly, they had a genuinely better time learning. Ensuring that *all* my students knew I cared deeply about them (especially the ones who needed it the most), using the right communication skills to hold them accountable and to deepen connections, and building in connection rituals and games that elicited positive emotions and a sense of belonging led to an authentically equitable classroom environment for my students.

Communicate to Connect: Strategies That Strengthen Relationships

In the next sections, you'll get many practical tools to use with groups of students and with individuals. We'll start with the pillars of attuned communication to set a strong foundation for the rest of the skills. Then we'll delve into a simple approach that allows us to navigate conflict easily. We will then learn about relational bids, followed by two powerful strategies to use when students have problems and when they cause you problems. Then you'll get another strategy for problem solving with students when everything else fails, as well as useful strategies to communicate with difficult parents. We'll conclude with practical activities and games to use in the classroom.

Connection and a sense of belonging are prerequisites for learning. When students know that their thoughts and emotions matter, they become active and engaged learners.

—Daniel Goleman

The Pillars of Attuned Communication

Before we explore how to talk so our students can listen, and how to listen so our students can talk, it's helpful to understand that the quality with which we approach relational dynamics is even more important than the words we use. If you incorporate the following elements into your conversations, you will naturally communicate in an attuned, emotionally intelligent way, and this will create more trust and connection with your students as well as your own loved ones.

The six pillars of attuned communication are: drop in with presence, notice nonverbal cues, get curious, reflect back, empathize, and acknowledge.

DROPPING IN WITH PRESENCE

NOTICING NONVERBAL CUES

BEING CURIOUS

REFLECTING BACK

EMPATHIZING

ACKNOWLEDGING

Drop In with Presence

When you listen to your student, colleague, parent, or loved one, as much as possible, fully drop into the conversation by being completely present. Be there and be there. This means shifting your body to be right next to the person or squarely in front of them. Then, mentally drop everything else so you can focus on the other person's experience.

With this level of presence, mindfully discern whether it is time for you to speak or time for you to listen. This will help the conversation flow and allow the other person to feel more seen and heard.

Questions to ask yourself about your level of presence:

- On a scale of 1 to 10, how present am I in this conversation?
- Am I hearing what is not said (the message underneath the words)?
- Would it be better for me to listen or talk at this juncture of the conversation?

Notice Nonverbal Cues

I used to work with a principal who deeply wanted to be liked by her teachers, yet most of us felt intimidated by her because when she looked at us, she would devour us with her eyes. On top of that, she would usually stand quite close to whoever she talked to, her tone of voice was overly assertive, and when she shook hands, she would squeeze so hard that it hurt. She was very well meaning and wanted to establish rapport, but she ended up alienating people and was confused by that. She was principal for a short time.

Whether you are aware of it or not, when you communicate with others, nonverbal cues are flying back and forth rapidly and constantly. Your facial expressions, posture, gestures, tone of voice, and eye contact send stronger messages than your words do. According to Albert Mehrabian, a researcher of body language, 55 percent of communication is nonverbal, 38 percent is vocal (as in tone of voice), and only 7 percent comes from the content of words spoken.[7] Nonverbal cues show the other person how interested you are in their experience, whether you're being honest, and whether you care about them. The acronym FIESTAS summarizes the seven categories of nonverbal communication:

Facial expression
Intonation
Eye contact
Sounds
Touch
Actions
Spaciousness

FACIAL EXPRESSION: When we smile, frown, roll our eyes, or move the muscles in our face to convey that we're surprised, fearful, sad, or are experiencing empathy for the other person, we send very strong messages to that person. It's helpful to keep in mind that people are interpreting our expressions.

INTONATION: When you speak, other people interpret your tone of voice in addition to your words. They notice how loud you are, the inflection of your voice, where you put your emphasis, and the timing and pacing of your speech. The simple phrase "Jonny, have a seat" can convey vastly different messages to a student depending on the tone used by the teacher.

EYE CONTACT: Connecting eye to eye with someone else for a split second communicates that you want to see them and that you are present with them. It sends a strong message of "you are not a number," "I see you," and "I'm here for you."

SOUNDS: Sounds like "ah" and "uh-huh" show the person that you are following what they are saying. "Hmm" can convey empathy, curiosity, or questioning, depending on the tone of voice. We can choose sounds intentionally to deepen connection.

TOUCH: Research shows that physical touch can play an important role in building connection. A pat on the back or shoulder, a warm hug, or a high five all send strong messages. Because we want every student to feel safe, and given that some may suffer from physical abuse at home or may be neurologically different or may simply not want to be touched, it is crucial to attune to their need for space and provide it. Explicitly asking for consent before touching a student goes a long way toward establishing trust. You can simply ask, "Would you like a hug?" or "High five?" Alternatively, instead of touching their body, you can touch their desk as you sit next to them.

ACTIONS: Noticing slight hand gestures or the position of someone's arms, torso, or head can give us a clue as to whether the listener is leaning in or needs a break. The way we sit and stand can also communicate a lot. Are you seated with your hands folded, leaning backward? If so, the other person is likely going to believe that you are closed and uninterested, or perhaps even fearful of what they are saying. However if you lean in, your arms are at your side, and your head is straight, they will immediately feel seen because they can sense your engagement.

SPACE: Have you ever had someone invade your personal space or tower over you? That's awkward at best. Appropriate proximity conveys a sense of attunement and respect for the other person. If the student is sitting and you are standing up, kneel down to get to their eye level or sit next to them.

Get Curious

Curiosity is the level of interest that you have in another person's experience. That level changes depending on how rushed we feel, how long we've known the person, and how important they are to us.

Sometimes students need to be heard, patiently, and when we show them that we truly care by asking follow-up questions to get to the essence of their experience, it builds trust and deepens connection because it sends this message: "I'm not only listening to you; I deeply care about your experience and want to make sure I understand it more completely."

Ask yourself, on a scale of 1 to 10, how genuinely curious you are about this person's experience. Be honest with yourself. This is not a leading question. If you find yourself to be at a 1, it tells you that this relationship, at this particular moment, is not as important to you as something else. That's very good information to have. If a student wants to share something with you and your curiosity level about their experience is low because you feel rushed or are exhausted, then you can ask them to approach you with their issue after class or during a tutorial so you can have time to be more present and more curious.

Sometimes students or colleagues need to be heard right away. If this is the case, and if you can listen to them but aren't feeling very curious about their experience, first fully accept that this is where you are. Then ask yourself whether you can be slightly more curious for just two more minutes, as this can make a massive difference in understanding someone's experience.

As teachers, we often think that we know what our students' problems are, when in fact we don't. And the longer you teach, the easier it is to put kids into categories. This kid needs more boundaries, this kid responds to humor, this kid needs more gentleness, and this kid needs to be challenged. On the one hand, categorizing saves us time and allows us to support many students in a classroom environment. But for it to work really well, our assumptions about students' needs must be correct, which is not always the case.

Sentence stems for getting curious about the other person:

- Tell me more about . . .
- I'm curious about . . .
- Ooh! I'd love to know more about . . .
- What's the hardest part about . . .
- What's your concern?

Being curious about someone must come from a place of genuine desire to get to know them, not from a place of judgment or interrogation. Most people (including kids) will pick up on it right away if you have an agenda behind your questions or if you want to steer them in a certain direction.

Reflect Back

Reflecting back means repeating or paraphrasing what the other person just shared with you. It shows them that when you were listening to them, you weren't thinking about what you were going to say next. Instead, you were so fully present with them that you are able to reflect back what you heard them say. This also helps you gauge whether you indeed heard them correctly, and it allows you to avoid misunderstandings that can drain your time and energy.

Sentence stems for describing what you're hearing the other person saying:

- What I hear you say is . . .
- If I hear you right, you're saying . . .?
- Is it accurate to say . . .?
- You are feeling (repeat back feelings that you heard them say).
- I noticed (inarguable fact) happened.
- I noticed that (inarguable expectation) wasn't met.

Empathize

Theresa Wiseman, a nurse and an empathy scholar, believes that there are four components to empathy:[8]

- Being nonjudgmental
- Recognizing that someone else's perspective is their truth
- Recognizing their emotions and understanding how that person experiences them
- Communicating your understanding of their feelings and validating them

Empathy is about understanding and connecting without fixing things. It's about sitting with someone else and putting connection first, above all else. It's realizing that when people feel fully understood, they are a lot more likely to come up with natural solutions to their own problems. Empathy leads to empowerment.

> It's important to remember that we cannot know with 100 percent certainty what the other person feels because we are not them.

It's important to remember that we cannot know with 100 percent certainty what the other person feels because we are not them. So try to avoid saying things like "I know exactly how you feel right now" or "I totally get what you're going through." Even if these sentences are meant to be supportive, they are not honoring the fact that the person in front of you is different and is experiencing the world in a different way than you do.

Combined with curiosity, empathy allows us to serve our students and support our colleagues in the best possible way because those two components give us the information we need to understand how to help. Without them, we're blind to what our students need and we teach to the needs of the "average" student. The only problem is that "average" students don't actually exist.

Sentence stems for empathizing with the other person:

- I imagine that you're feeling (actual feeling, not thought).
- I imagine that you're thinking (repeat thoughts they share).
- I can hear how (emotion they are experiencing) you are feeling.
- I can hear in your voice that . . .
- It sounds like you might be feeling . . .
- I sense that you are feeling (emotion they are experiencing).
- That sounds like a (adjective) experience.
- That sounds (adjective).

You can check whether you understood their experience correctly by saying: "I imagine . . ." and following up with "Is it true?" (And prepare to be OK with being wrong since that gives you great information as well.)

For a deeper dive into the importance of slowing down to empathize, scan the QR code.

Acknowledge

Acknowledgment is naming something that you find to be true about the other person. You can acknowledge a behavior, an accomplishment, or a character trait. Remember this: what people want the most in life, after they have shelter, food, and basic necessities, is to feel seen, to feel understood, and to belong. It is amazing how fast people bond when one person feels seen and acknowledged by the other.

> What people want the most in life, after they have shelter, food, and basic necessities, is to feel seen, to feel understood, and to belong.

The result of acknowledging our students is that they are a lot more likely to focus, to do what we ask of them, and to behave in a way that works for us and the other students.

To be meaningful and effective, and to avoid turning a student into a praise-seeking individual, the acknowledgment should have the following components: it should be worth giving, specific, sincere, and concise.

WORTH GIVING: Be intentional with your acknowledgments or praise, and only give them when they are deserved.

SPECIFIC: The more specific you can be about a behavior you want to acknowledge, the better. For example: "The way you told Ernesto to stop talking to you during quiet reading time was great. You were clear and respectful, and you asserted your need. That was impressive." While it is OK to just say "Good job" from time to time, ask yourself what you are specifically praising, and then share that explicitly in your acknowledgment.

SINCERE: Students can smell bullshit from miles away, and if your acknowledgment or praise is not genuine, it can actually do damage if the student thinks you're being sarcastic or manipulative. Before acknowledging a student, check in with yourself. Are you moved by what you are seeing and do you have a real desire to share that with them? They will sense the excitement underneath your words, which is often more important than the words themselves.

CONCISE: How easy is it for you to receive acknowledgments or praise from others? For most people, it's difficult, and if you're honest with yourself, you might realize the same is true for you. Try to keep your acknowledgments to a sentence or two at most. They will be easier for your students to take in.

Examples:

> A student is showing you how dedicated they are to improving their writing skills by meeting with you a number of times during office hours.
>
> **ACKNOWLEDGMENT:** "Monisha, I have to tell you that I'm very impressed by your grit and your commitment to improving your writing skills."
>
> A student is helping another student in class who is feeling overwhelmed.

ACKNOWLEDGMENT: "Tina, I noticed that you saw that Sumeet seemed overwhelmed and you reached out to help him. You have a knack for caring about others and helping them. That's beautiful."

A student is upset with a grade that they earned on a test.

ACKNOWLEDGMENT: "I get how much you care about succeeding in school, Tommy. That's a really good thing. I also get that earning this grade is disappointing for you."

In this last scenario, many teachers would be tempted to try to "fix" their student's emotions by saying, "Don't worry, there will be other tests and you can raise your grade." While well meaning, this statement can feel dismissive and cause more distance. Simply sharing the acknowledgment above shows the student that you see and understand them. It is a form of active listening, which cultivates a deeper bond between you two, which increases the likelihood that your student will work to improve their mastery of the material moving forward.

Note the four elements in each of these examples: worth giving, specific, sincere, and concise.

Sentence stems for acknowledging the other person:

- Thank you for . . .
- I appreciate the way you . . .
- I feel your care for . . .
- I can see that . . .
- Your ability to . . .
- I appreciate your courage in bringing this up.
- I'm impressed by your (resilience, care, self-awareness, etc.).

The pillars of attuned communication deepen relationships when everything is going well in the classroom as well as when problems arise. While we would all love to live in a utopia, as long as we put people in a room together, problems can arise. Why? Because teachers are humans with needs, goals, and limited energy. And so are students.

How Most Conflicts Arise and How to Easily Avoid Them

When we are in a relationship with someone, we make observations about them, we make assumptions about them based on our observations, and we draw conclusions based on our assumptions. Psychologists call that the ladder of inference.[9] Observations lead to assumptions, which lead to conclusions. Conflicts occur when people make the wrong assumptions about other people's behaviors.

You observe a student arriving late to your class for a third time, you assume they are late because they were talking to their friends, and you conclude that they don't care about you or your class. You observe that your colleague is having a side chat with another colleague while you are addressing a group of your colleagues, you assume that they are talking about you, and you conclude that they are disrespectful. You see your partner come home with six burritos for dinner when you only have four people in your family, you assume that they don't care about conserving food or paying attention to your family budget, and you conclude that they are wasteful. And every time one of these people exhibits the same behavior, it reinforces your conclusion about who they are. Your student is late again, and your mind says: "That's so like Jenny. She is always late!"

Of course, each of these people has a ladder of inference of their own. Your student observes that she has little time to connect with friends she cares about deeply, she assumes that there is no impact on you or your classroom if she is late, and she concludes that showing up late is OK. Your colleague observes that you are leading a meeting, she assumes it would be disruptive to ask you a pressing question, and she concludes that it is less disruptive to ask a colleague nearby. Your partner observes that he's in charge of making sure there's food for

Teacher Conclusion:
"Jenny doesn't value me
or my class"

CONCLUSIONS

Student Conclusion:
"It's OK if I'm slightly late"

Teacher Assumption:
"Jenny cares more about
socializing with friends
than being on time"

ASSUMPTIONS

Student Assumption:
"She/he doesn't notice/care
if I'm late by a min or two"

Teacher Observation:
"Jenny is late again"

OBSERVATIONS

Student Observation:
"Teacher is teaching more
than 30 students"

everyone, he assumes more food is better because he comes from a family that experienced scarcity, and he concludes that the most loving thing he can do is buy six burritos for four people.

When we are in destructive conflict with others, we argue only about our conclusions and we fail to name our inferences. "You're wasteful!" "What? I'm not wasteful, I'm caring!" These conflicts can quickly escalate. If instead we share our observations and assumptions by naming our inferences, and we invite the other person to do the same, we can often avoid the conflict altogether or have a constructive conflict that brings us closer.

> When we are in destructive conflict with others, we argue only about our conclusions and we fail to name our inferences.

It's important to know that in any healthy relationship, conflict will and should occur. The goal isn't to avoid conflict; the goal is to navigate conflict in a way that allows everyone to be seen and understood. By doing this, both parties can grow from the experience, solve the conflict, and, if possible, deepen the relationship.

When I was in my second year of teaching, I gave my students a unit test, and upon grading it, I felt frustrated because I thought they should have earned better grades. Of course, a little bit of introspection would have led me to realize that I didn't do a good enough job of teaching the material on the test, but instead I fell into the trap of comparing my students' grades with those of my colleagues' students. It wasn't pretty, and I started to come up with excuses. I remembered one particular girl telling me she didn't get much out of studying for hours at home and that she didn't mind not having stellar grades. In retrospect, I find her approach healthier than that of the type A personalities at the school. But I couldn't see this at the time, and I used that information to rationalize why she got a bad score and to justify my frustration with her.

The next day, after passing the graded tests back to my students, I asked that girl to stay after class to chat about what happened. After the bell rang and the rest of the students left, I said to her, "Studying is an important part of the class, and it's important that you apply yourself. Why didn't you study more for this test?" And to this day, I will never forget her reply. This fourteen-year-old looked me straight in the eyes and, without missing a beat, asked, "Why didn't you teach us the material properly?" Ouch! I was so shocked that I had no response, and the student left.

What just happened? I was trying to show this student that I believed in her, and this was how she responded? Well, yes, because I made a fatal error in my communication that almost cost me all the social capital I'd built with her that year. I did not name my inference.

Naming Our Inferences: a Simple Three-Step Approach

Naming our inferences is taking responsibility for our feelings and thoughts; noticing our observations, assumptions, and conclusions; explicitly sharing that our assumptions are indeed assumptions; and then checking to see if these assumptions are actually true.

> Most people mindlessly believe that their assumptions about others are true.

Most people mindlessly believe that their assumptions about others are true, and that leads them to create stories in their heads to justify their position. The trap of believing that you know what another person is thinking or feeling, or why they behave as they do, is the primary cause for tension, misunderstanding, and disconnection in relationships.

Naming inferences is important because when you name your inference, you give others the space to take responsibility for their behaviors and thoughts, and you allow them the opportunity to name their own inference. This also gives students more space to take charge of their own learning.

When I asked my student why she hadn't studied more for the test, I backed her into a corner. I didn't give her any room to consider what actually led her to earn a poor grade on the test. I made an assumption about her and treated it as if it were a fact that she needed to accept. This student happened to be a fighter, so instead of collapsing or shutting down, as soon as she felt backed into a corner, she responded defensively. And can you blame her? I didn't give her the space to *not* be defensive. If I had named my inference, the conversation would have gone very differently.

How do we name our inference? We can use a simple yet profound three-step communication system that is virtually foolproof if used correctly.

Step 1: Describe the Inarguable Facts

The first step is to describe what you notice about the other person or hear the other person say. Importantly, *notice* or *hear* means pointing out what is inarguable. You start the sentence by saying: "I notice that . . ." or "What I'm hearing you say is . . ." The rest of the sentence has to be inarguable. As in "I notice that you yawned three times today in class" as opposed to "I notice that you are tired." You are making the assumption that they are tired, but it's not inarguable.

Sometimes it's OK to notice things outside of the relational dynamic. For example, I could have said: "I noticed that you earned a sixty-eight on your test" or "I noticed that you lowered your head and put your hand on it when I passed the test back to you."

You may even share what you notice about your inner experience: "I notice that I'm concerned about the grade you earned on the test." Since this is *your* experience, it is inarguable.

Step 2: Confirm That You're Making an Assumption

The second step is to make an assumption based on what you noticed and to tell the individual that you are making an assumption. You can start a sentence with "I imagine . . ." to communicate the following to the other person: "I acknowledge that I can never know what your experience is like, but you are important enough to me that I am trying to imagine and empathize with what might be going on for you." The key here is to not worry about whether you are right or wrong but instead to approach the assumption with curiosity and to give yourself the permission to be wrong.

In this case, I could have said: "I noticed that you earned a sixty-eight on your test, and I imagine that you didn't feel the need to study much for this test" or "I imagine that you are disappointed by the grade you earned."

Instead of "I imagine," you could use "I have this story in my head that . . ." For example: "I noticed that you earned a sixty-eight on your test, and I'm making up a story in my head that you might not have studied enough for it."

Step 3: Check If Your Assumption Is True

The third step is crucial: check whether your assumption is true and be prepared to accept whatever answer comes your way. You can do this by ending your statement with a simple question: "Is it true?" These three words tell the other person that this is really a dialogue between you two, that you are their ally, that you are simply trying to understand their reality, and that you are prepared to be wrong if that is the case.

I NOTICE   I IMAGINE   IS IT TRUE?

These three steps give the student space to reflect on the actual problem instead of deciding whether to fight you or flee from you. They also model to the student how to name their own inference.

Imagine if I had said this to my student: "Hey, so I noticed that you earned a sixty-eight on your test, and I imagine that you didn't feel the need to study much for this test. Is that true?" She would have had nothing to push against and would have had space to ponder that question.

In some cases, more sensitive students might still feel backed into a corner, so you could soften your statement: "Hey, I wanted to connect with you because I noticed that you earned a sixty-eight on your test. I'm telling myself a story that you didn't feel the need to study much for this test. To be honest, I'm really not sure whether my story is true or not. Is it true?" By explicitly saying that you are telling yourself a story (which you are), you show the other person that you are prepared for your story to be wrong.

The beautiful part of this process is that if a student tells you that you're wrong, that they did actually study a good amount for a test, you could follow up with additional questions, such as: "Did you feel like you understood the material when you studied for it?" And now, instead of getting into a battle about whether they studied enough, you are on your way to actual learning.

Sometimes it's quite difficult to name our inference, especially when you have to deal with a colleague or a parent who drives you nuts or whom you fear for one reason or another. For an example of how to name our inference effectively with a difficult person, scan the QR code.

Identify and State Your Positive Intentions

In one day of school, there are hundreds of opportunities to correct students' behavior. "Don't hit your classmate, don't distract others, don't forget to do your homework," etc. It's easy for us to express what we don't want to see, but it's helpful to turn this around into what we do want to see and then to intentionally state that. "I want you to keep yourself and others safe," or "I want you to succeed, so let's talk about focusing in class and doing your homework." The benefit of identifying and stating your positive intention is that it lets the other person know where you want to go. This is particularly important when we are in a conflict because it orients the conversation toward a possibility. It builds a frame for the conversation. Remember that what seems obvious to you is not necessarily obvious to your student.

It's easy for us to express what we don't want to see, but it's helpful to turn this around into what we do want to see and then to intentionally state that.

Turning Toward Our Students

Dr. John Gottman has shown that one of the most important skills adults can develop in their relationships with other adults and with children is to be able to notice others' bids for attention and "turn toward" them at that moment.[10] A bid for attention is an attempt to get acceptance, affection, or emotional connection. A classic example is when a child asks their parent, "Will you play with me?" There are three ways the parent can respond: they can turn toward, which builds emotional connectedness; they can turn away, which creates disconnection; or they can provide no response, which is another form of turning away. The second and third types of response usually lead to dysregulation for both parties.

Turning toward does not mean that the parent decides to play with the child. The mother could say: "Oh, sweetie, I wish that I could play with you, as that is one of my favorite things to do. I can't now, but I'll be ready to play after I finish working, around six o'clock. I'm looking forward to it!" The research shows that the more we turn toward others, the more we fill up what Gottman calls their *emotional bank accounts*. Before we look at how to apply this concept in the classroom, it's important to understand one more fact about what leads relationships to thrive.

Emotional Bank Accounts and the Positivity Ratio

In every healthy relationship there will be some conflict and moments of hurt and disconnection. The key is to know how to experience the conflict in a healthy way and to understand that thriving relationships have a much greater number of positive interactions than difficult ones. Each positive interaction with a person is a deposit in their emotional bank account. Each difficult interaction is a withdrawal from their emotional bank account.

The difference between a regular bank account and an emotional bank account is that a withdrawal (turning away) in an emotional bank account has a much greater weight than a deposit (turning toward).[11] In the context of romantic relationships, Gottman found that, on average, a couple needs five positive interactions to one negative interaction.[12] Meaning that couples who thrive have at least a five-to-one ratio, but they usually have a ten-to-one or even twenty-to-one ratio. These positive interactions are often small and simple, such as sending an encouraging or loving text, hugging before going to work, holding hands while going on a walk, cooking for each other, laughing about something together, looking into each other's eyes, and showing appreciation for positive gestures.

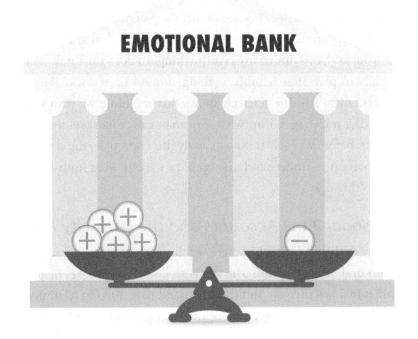

The same idea applies in the context of parenting, and psychologist Marcial Losada found that at work, teams that thrive also have at least a six-to-one ratio of positive interactions to negative interactions.[13] Note that the ratio is not six to zero, meaning that some conflict, even passionate conflict, is necessary for a team or for a marriage to thrive, but the vast majority of interaction must be positive for a team to succeed.

In the context of teaching, the concept of the positivity ratio is key to creating a thriving classroom climate. In practical terms, no educator can keep track of how many positive interactions to difficult interactions they have had with each student. Luckily that is not the goal. The goal is to create an environment and model communication skills that facilitate a five-to-one ratio of positive interactions to negative interactions for most individuals in the classroom.

Noticing our students' bids for attention will go a long way toward that, and I have provided some examples of bids below. I also present activities such as improv games, connection rituals, and mindfulness practices at the end of chapters 2 through 7 of this book, and I present communication strategies in this chapter. Together, these practices will help you fill students' emotional bank accounts and ensure a high enough positivity ratio. This not only allows for students to thrive, but it also makes teaching so much easier because students' brains are primed and ready to learn.

Examples of obvious bids for attention:

- Student raises their hand
- Student asks for help
- Student says hi to you in the morning
- Student asks, "What do you think of my (drawing, story, essay, worksheet)?"
- Student always wants to be first to share
- Student stands next to you quietly until you acknowledge them
- Student interrupts other students
- Student interrupts you

Examples of nonobvious bids:

- Student doesn't show up to class three days in a row (or consistently misses one or two days a week)
- Student doesn't turn in their homework for three days in a row
- Student asks to go to the bathroom regularly during your class
- Student asks to go to the nurse more often than usual, experiencing somatic illnesses (headache, stomachache)

Responding to Positive Bids

You naturally respond to positive bids all day long without even recognizing it. Saying yes in response to a student raising their hand. Replying with "Hi, how are you?" when a student says hi to you. Laughing at a student's joke. But what about when we don't have time? How can we still turn toward the student while setting a boundary so that we can continue to focus on what we need to in that moment? Here are some examples:

- "So glad you have your hand up. I can't help you now but will do so when I can!"
- "I wish I could talk to you now. I really need to tend to something else, but I'll get back to you." (Do your best to actually remember to get back to them.)
- "I'd love to look at your (essay, story, drawing), and I'm not able to right now. Let's make sure we do it after class!" (Or whenever is convenient for you.)

If you can't respond verbally, take half a second to turn toward the student, establish eye contact with them, and raise your index finger to indicate that they need to wait. If you can have a warm and gentle smile on your face, all the better.

To the best of your ability, avoid ignoring the student altogether for a long time, and avoid yelling or criticizing the student for wanting your attention. I know, it's easier said than done, but it is doable. And remember that the more you model caring, attuned, and respectful communication, the more likely your students are to give that back to you.

Responding to Difficult Bids and Holding Students Accountable

What do you do with the kid who is constantly asking for your attention and doesn't recognize that there is a whole class you have to teach? Here's how you can turn toward students when they ask for attention in maladaptive ways:

- Make them feel important by giving them an important task.
- Give them time to talk in groups so they can let off some "attention" steam.
- When they create a problem for you or continually interrupt others, send them a clear I-message. (We'll delve into how to do that in the next section.)
- Offer them a choice: "You can stay in the class and respect others, or you can take a few minutes to be with yourself in our peaceful zone or outside the class" (if you have an aide who can be with them).
- Meet with the student outside of class, explain to them that while you would love to always be able to answer their questions, you can't because you have thirty other students. Then come up with a nonverbal sign, using hands or fingers, that can belong to just the two of you. It will signal that you are not able to pay attention to them now but that you will get back to them when you're available.
- Recognize that in some instances, students who constantly make bids for attention do it because they are chronically

anxious. Teaching these students to self-soothe is the best long-term solution for you and for them. I go over these strategies in the next chapter of the book.

Holding a student accountable can sometimes be seen by them as a negative interaction. They may think, "Why are you picking on me?" But when we respond in a firm yet caring way, saying: "I'm doing this because I care about you and I believe you can succeed," we turn toward them.

A crucial point to make here is that if you've already shown students you genuinely care about cultivating a relationship with them, you will be exponentially more successful at holding them accountable. That's because if they've felt an emotional connection with you in the past, they are much more likely to believe that you actually mean it when you tell them, "I care about you and I believe you can succeed, and that's why I'm holding you accountable." And they are also more likely to internalize that message, look at their maladaptive behavior, learn a lesson, and grow.

> If you've already shown students you genuinely care about cultivating a relationship with them, you will be exponentially more successful at holding them accountable.

Even if you respond perfectly to your students' bids, and even if you name your inferences, problems will still arise in the classroom. There are simple yet powerful strategies for these moments. That's the topic of the next section.

Simple and Powerful Methods That Solve Classroom Problems

Rarely does a response make something better.
What makes something better is connection.

—Brené Brown

The concepts and skills in the following paragraphs come from a wonderful book written by Thomas Gordon called *Teacher Effectiveness Training*.[14] I took what I believed to be the most important tools for dealing with the reality that teachers face today and infused them with current examples.

In the book, Gordon shares a simple yet powerful graphic organizer that shows how time and attention in the classroom are always divided into three sections: the teaching and learning zone, the students' problems zone, and the teacher problems zone.

THE TEACHER PROBLEMS ZONE	THE TEACHING AND LEARNING ZONE	THE STUDENTS' PROBLEMS ZONE

While the ideal scenario would be for the learning zone to take up most of the rectangle, the size of each zone varies depending on the class you teach and the issues the students bring with them. To address the problems in our classroom and turn them into learning opportunities, we first need to be able to distinguish between the problems owned by students and the problems owned by the teacher. The approach we need to take is different for each type of problem.

To ascertain whether a problem is owned by you or a student, ask yourself the following questions: "Is this behavior affecting me directly?

Is it interfering with my teaching? Is it hurting me or my performance in any way? Is it physically hurting another student?" If the answer to any of those questions is yes, then you own the problem. If the answer to all of them is no, then the student owns the problem.

Here are some examples of problems in the classroom. See if you can classify them as student owned or teacher owned.

1. Student is tapping her pencil constantly
2. Student is anxious about the upcoming test
3. Student carved his initials onto a desk
4. Student is visibly upset and slumps quietly in her chair
5. Student is on his cell phone laughing while you're giving instructions
6. Student is overwhelmed by the amount of homework

Numbers 1, 3, and 5 are teacher-owned problems. Numbers 2, 4, and 6 are student-owned problems.

How to Respond when a Problem Is Owned by the Student

Imagine a student says this: "I don't know what to do about the test that's coming next week. Even though I study for your tests, I always do badly because you always give such difficult tests." It would be very tempting for you to reply defensively: "No I don't, all you have to do is study more!" Or you might be dismissive: "Relax, as long as you study correctly for it, you'll be fine." It might even be tempting to question their logic: "Are you sure you are studying correctly? If you did, the test would be easy." While it is a perfectly good idea to look into how the student is studying for the test, the problem with these responses is that they are guaranteed to either turn students off or to increase their level of stress, not decrease it. In other words, you've made the situation worse, and it will be more difficult for the student to learn the material because their nervous system is even less regulated than it was in the first place.

Examples of ineffective communication "strategies" are:

- Ordering: "Stop worrying about this and get to work."
- Warning: "It's time to start focusing or else you might very well fail the class."
- Should-ing: "You should leave your personal problems at home where they belong."
- Solution Giving: "You just need to go to sleep an hour earlier and stop playing video games!" Or "You should have an easier class load." Or "You should not play with this student."
- Fact Giving: "Don't forget that three-quarters of your grade is yet to be determined."
- Criticizing: "Develop a tougher skin!" Or "Don't be so sensitive."
- Name Calling: "Why are you behaving like a toddler right now?"
- Praising: "You are such a smart student! I'm not worried about you."
- Rationalizing: "Everyone feels overwhelmed from time to time. You got this!"
- Questioning: "Why are you telling me this only now?"
- Dismissing: "It's not that bad, is it? Come on, you're fine."

You likely don't use most of these, but if you're honest with yourself and self-reflective enough, you will probably find that you engage in at least one of them to some degree. I encourage you to point that out to yourself and to be kind and gentle with yourself when you do. Then get curious and ask yourself, "Why do I do that? Where did I pick that up? Am I ready to shift away from that?"

Why are these ways of communicating damaging?

When we talk to students, we often send multiple messages to them. The verbal message and the "hidden" but just as powerful message. For example, imagine a student tells you this: "I don't understand why adults have to be so rigid with their rules all the time. My parents are super strict, my teachers have their rules, I'm sick of it!" You might respond: "Yeah, I get it, lots of teenagers feel this way. You'll understand when you grow up and you're a parent, trust me. Don't get too worked up about it." But the student is likely to pick up on a much stronger message behind your words: "My teacher doesn't think my feelings are valid, he thinks that I'm too young and stupid to really understand how the world works, he is not interested in my feelings about this, and he doesn't get me." Note that however well meaning you may be, your response can generate relational distance and dissonance.

So am I telling you that you can never praise, question, disagree with, order, or offer solutions to a student?

Not at all. If you are in the learning zone—the no-problem area—you can communicate a lot more freely. I still encourage you to stick to the pillars of attuned communication, but in the learning zone you can (and sometimes should) offer solutions, crack jokes, or give orders such as "Please sit down, we're about to start." But remember that I'm recommending you avoid these when students are distressed, upset with themselves, anxious, stressed, or feeling shame. Just think about the last time you were in distress and decided to get some support from a friend. If your friend was dismissive or judgmental, if they told you how you should have behaved or offered unwanted solutions, if they pitied you or questioned your feelings about what you shared, how did that make you feel? And more importantly, what kind of response would you have liked to receive? While some of us would want solutions to our problems, we would first want to know that we were fully seen and understood by our friend.

So, what strategies should we use for a student-owned problem?

The name of the game is connection. You want to lower a student's stress or anxiety level by showing them that you fully get their emotional experience and that you understand all emotions are valid (though not all thoughts or all behavior).

Before we delve into strategies in more detail, keep in mind that our attitude is more important than our words.

The Mindset That We Need to Be In

The mindset we need for these conversations has four components:

1. Remember that students are often more resilient than we imagine. Believe that ultimately they will be able to solve their own problems. It may take them longer than we want, but it's important to resist the temptation to fix this for them. Our role is to empower them to fix their own problems. Over time this will actually save us time and energy.

2. Remember that a student's experience and feelings are valid regardless of whether we think they should feel differently. We need to authentically accept and validate their feelings.

   We don't need to validate their thoughts or maladaptive behaviors, but if we believe that their feelings are inappropriate, we risk sending a nonverbal signal that we don't accept them. When feelings arise, they are simply there; it's senseless to analyze whether a person should have them or not.

3. Remember that all feelings are temporary, and they move along faster when we name them—and especially when we genuinely accept them. They arise, are felt, get diffused, and pass.

4. We must hold space for the student but not get hijacked by their feelings. Our empathy should lead to a place of compassion, but we must not lose ourselves in their distress.

Once we are in the right mindset, we can use one of (or a combination of) the following powerful strategies:

Listen Attentively in Silence

Most of us underestimate the power of listening to others in silence and holding space for them to express themselves. Silence can feel uncomfortable for us, yet a student cannot express what is really going on for them if you do most of the talking. If you don't have something useful

When feelings arise, they are simply there; it's senseless to analyze whether a person should have them or not.

to say, or if the other person is so upset that they must downregulate before they can take in information, it's an especially good idea for you to give them space.

For example, if a student is upset because they earned a bad grade on a test, restraining yourself from saying something just to fill the gap is a powerful learned skill to possess. It's particularly hard to restrain yourself if you are triggered by the situation or what your student has said. But remember that if the other person is unable to take in what you're saying, your words will not be heard and will likely create distance between you two.

Provide an Empathic Sound, Word, or Phrase

If you remain silent for too long, students may feel that you're not following what they're saying. Try responding to what they share with "ah," "mmm," "uh-huh," "wow," "that's hard," "I see," or "gosh." This helps the students to feel that you understand what they're telling you.

Invite Them to Share More

When students fall silent for a moment, ask them: "Is there more?" or "Is something else on your mind?" or "Want to share more about this?" If a student is silent but something is clearly going on, all it takes is a simple invitation to share: "Want to talk about it?" or "What's up?" or "I'm here if you want to talk."

Example of what this type of communication looks like:

> Student: I don't know what to do about the test that's coming next week. Even though I study for your tests, I always do badly because you always give such difficult tests.
>
> Teacher: Oh, tell me more.
>
> Student: I just know how difficult your tests are and whatever I do to study never works.
>
> Teacher: That's hard.

Student: Yeah, it's really hard. It makes me want to give up and not study at all.

Teacher: I see.

Student: So I'm not sure what to do.

Teacher: Uh-huh. (Wait for the student to think about what they should do. Do not jump in to fix their problem.)

Student: I guess maybe studying differently will help, but I don't know how.

Teacher: Want to share more about this?

Student: Sure, I just spend hours studying my notes and memorizing all these facts and then I get to the test and forget it all.

Teacher: I see.

At this point, the teacher could suggest new ways of studying, new test-taking strategies, etc. Note that by providing simple cues of attuned listening and not jumping in to save the student right away, the student has an opportunity to come up with the solution and the teacher has a lot more information to work with. Also note the teacher's skill in not getting defensive after the student's first sentence.

With all of that said, sometimes we need to show our students that we're following what they're saying *and* we're actively imagining what they're feeling in an attempt to fully understand what they're going through. That's when active listening comes in handy.

Use Active Listening

Active listening involves:

1. Identifying and naming thoughts and feelings
2. Restating or paraphrasing some of what was shared
3. Accepting feelings and reasserting boundaries

Let's take the previous example of the worried student.

She says: "I don't know what to do about the test that's coming next week. Even though I study for your tests, I always do badly because you always give such difficult tests."

You could identify and name her feelings by saying: "Sounds like you are worried about the next test and feel hopeless because you didn't do as well as you wished on previous tests, even though you studied for them." (Strategy #1.)

The student might then respond with: "Yes, the tests are so hard and I always bomb them, even though I swear that I study for them!"

To which you could respond with: "Hmm . . . I see" or "That's gotta be tough." (Empathic sound, word, or phrase.)

The student might then say: "It is! It's like all my effort goes to nothing and I just want to give up."

You can paraphrase what they just shared by saying: "Sounds like you just want to give up because putting in effort doesn't lead to the results you were hoping for." (Strategy #2.)

The student might respond with: "Exactly! It's useless!"

To which you can respond by accepting her feelings and gently redirecting the conversation toward empowering the student to solve her own problem within boundaries that are acceptable to you. (Strategy #3.) You can say: "I get how frustrating and demoralizing it is to put effort into studying for a test and to earn a grade you're unhappy with. I would feel the same. I also get the desire to just give up. I believe in you and your ability to succeed in the class."

Notice that you are showing the student you fully accept her emotional experience. That will send her a message that you care. It will also make it easier for her to hear this next sentence and to be willing to brainstorm possible solutions with you: "While I'm not ready to change my expectations or my assessment, I'm wondering if you're open to brainstorming how *we* can help you succeed." Notice that this response strategically uses the pronoun "we" to reinforce collaboration.

Here are some more examples:

EXAMPLE #1: You've put students in stations to learn about the Civil War.

Student: This stuff is boring!

Teacher: Sounds like you're not interested in what we're doing now. Tell me more.

Student: I just can't get into it. I'm trying to read these paragraphs, but they are so dense and the information doesn't even make sense.

Teacher: You're trying to understand what you're reading and it's not making any sense. That's got to be frustrating and boring at the same time.

Student: Yeah, can I just do something else now?

Teacher: You really wish you didn't have to do this.

Student: Yep. Do I have to?

Teacher: Sounds like you would like me to make that decision for you.

Student: I mean, I know I'm supposed to . . . I just need some help.

Teacher: You need some help. Tell me more . . .

NOTE: Many new teachers believe that a student saying something is "boring" means it's the teacher's problem. It only becomes your problem if it interferes with your teaching. If many students say it's boring and they crack jokes with each other and interrupt the other students, then it becomes your problem to own.

EXAMPLE #2: You've assigned students to groups to work on a project together and one student insists on working alone.

Student: Can I just work by myself?

Teacher: You want to work by yourself. Can you share more about that?

Student: I just work better alone.

Teacher: Sounds like you feel more comfortable being by yourself.

Student: Yes.

Teacher: Uh-huh.

Student: So can I?

Teacher: Before I can tell you whether you can or not, I'd like to understand a bit more about why you want to work by yourself. What's hard about working with others?

Student: No one in this class likes me.

Teacher: Oh, you're upset because you think no one likes you.

Student: They don't. Tom made fun of me the other day and Jenny thinks I'm stupid.

Teacher: You're angry and hurt by some of the things that Tom and Jenny said to you.

Student: Yes! And I don't feel safe working with them.

Teacher: You feel unsafe working with them. Thanks for letting me know. It's important to me that people feel safe in this class. Tell you what, I'll address the situations with Tom and Jenny after class. For now, let's find a group that feels safe for you to work with.

EXAMPLE #3: A student puts their head down on their desk and slowly falls asleep. After giving the class instructions for a self-directed task, the teacher approaches the student's desk.

Teacher: I notice your head is on your desk. Can you tell me more about why that is?

Student (waking up): Oh, sorry, sorry, my bad.

Teacher: You feel bad for having your head on the desk.

Student: Yeah, I didn't mean it, I'm just really tired.

Teacher: Sounds like you're exhausted. Can you share more about that?

Student: Just didn't get much sleep last night, it's nothing personal. I like your class, I'm just tired.

Teacher: You are worried that I'll think you don't like my class.

Student: Yeah, but it's not that, I'm just tired is all.

Teacher: I hear that. Do you think you can stay alert in class now?

Student: Yes.

Teacher: Great. Ask one of your peers what we're working on now, and if you have any questions, let me know.

Important note: For some teachers (including my former self), a student putting their head down on their desk creates a teacher-owned problem because the teacher takes the student's behavior as a personal offense and they get distracted. If instead the interpretation is more neutral (like in the example above), the problem stays squarely with the student and the teacher can peacefully move on to teach the class. That requires having awareness of our interpretation of the external stimuli (in this case, the student putting their head on their desk).

WRITING EXERCISE: Think back to a time in the last week when a student owned a problem and you did not actively listen to them. Replay the dialogue in your head and ask yourself where in the conversation you could have actively listened to them. Journal about how you think the conversation would have gone. Then list three possible future moments in the next week when you could use active listening.

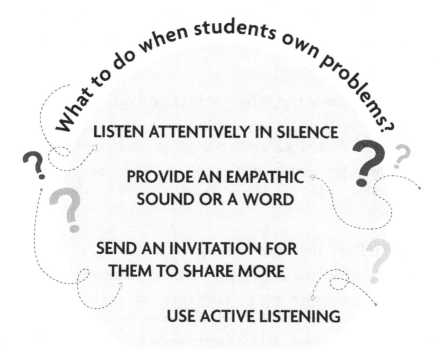

What to do when students own problems?

LISTEN ATTENTIVELY IN SILENCE

PROVIDE AN EMPATHIC SOUND OR A WORD

SEND AN INVITATION FOR THEM TO SHARE MORE

USE ACTIVE LISTENING

What About When a Student Is Creating a Problem for Me?

Instead of trying to control the student, send them an I-message that clearly explains how you are impacted.

There are three steps to sending an I-message.

Step 1: Describe What Is Unacceptable and Start the Sentence with "When"

Examples: "When you are on your cell phone" or "When you push others" or "When I get interrupted while giving instructions."

Note: Be careful not to add judgment and stay focused on the behavior. Avoid saying things like "When you are lazy" or "When you are disrespectful." These are you-messages. Ask yourself what specific behavior leads you to believe the student is lazy or disrespectful and focus on that.

Step 2: Express the Effect It Has on You

Examples: "When you are on your cell phone, I'm unable to have your attention" or "When you are on your cell phone, I need to expend more energy to refocus you on your task" or "When you are on your cell phone, I need to take the time to remind you of the school/classroom rules."

Step 3: Describe Your Feelings

Examples: "When you are on your cell phone, I need to take the time to remind you of the school/classroom rules, and I feel mad" or "If I get interrupted when I give instructions, I lose my train of thought and forget what I'm saying, and I feel very frustrated by that" or "When you push others, I need to ensure that everyone is safe and remind you of our classroom norms. I feel worried about others' safety and frustrated that I have to stop what I was doing."

NOTE: I-messages get the best responses when students can see that their behavior has a tangible effect on you or other students.

WRITING EXERCISE: Think back to a time in the last week when a student's (or group of students') behavior caused you a problem and write down an I-message that you could have sent them. Then use this I-message next time the student engages in that behavior and journal about how that interaction went. In what way was it different from past interactions?

Switching from I-Messages to Active Listening

After you send an I-message, even if it's perfectly delivered, the student may feel embarrassed, upset, surprised, sad, or maybe even defensive. Let's face it—no one likes finding out they have caused someone else a problem.

If you keep sending I-message after I-message in response to a defensive student, the exchange will lead to more distance. In this case, it's time for you to shift from an I-message back to active listening.

Example of sticking to I-messages without switching to active listening:

> Teacher: When I see and hear you pack your backpack before the bell rings, I get distracted and other students get distracted; it interrupts my train of thought, and it is very frustrating to me. (First I-message)
>
> Student: Yeah, well, your class is not the only class in the school, and my next class is far away, so I need to pack my bag in order to get there on time.
>
> Teacher: I get that, but when you make noise, I need to stop my teaching, which annoys me, and the passing period is long enough to get from class to class if you go straight to class. (Second I-message)
>
> Student: You try going straight to that classroom and make it on time. What's the big deal? I'm not making that much noise, and besides, I'm not the only one who is doing it!
>
> Teacher: When you dismiss what I have to say and speak to me in this tone, I feel disrespected and it makes me angry. (Third I-message)
>
> Student: Hey, I'm just stating the truth, there is no need for you to feel this way.

> Teacher: Don't tell me what to feel and what not to feel, you dis-
> respectful child! (You-message)

Because the teacher wanted to get his needs met right away, he forgot to listen to the student. It's not easy to respond to defensiveness with active listening, but it's the fastest way to get everyone's needs met while strengthening the relationship. Digging our heels in always exacerbates the problematic behavior.

Example of starting with an I-message and then switching to active listening:

> Teacher: When I see and hear you pack your backpack before the bell rings, I get distracted and other students get distracted; it interrupts my train of thought, and it is very frustrating to me. (First I-message)
> Student: Yeah, well, your class is not the only class in the school, and my next class is far away, so I need to pack my bag in order to get there on time.
> Teacher: Sounds like you are worried about not getting to your other class on time.
> Student: Yeah, these passing periods are way too short and I barely have time to say hi to any of my friends.
> Teacher: Got it. It's important for you to get to the other class on time and to be able to say hi to friends on your way over there.
> Student: Yes, I mean, I know that during passing periods I'm not meant to spend a lot of time talking to friends, and I don't. I just find it stressful to cross all of campus in such a short amount of time.
> Teacher: I see.
> Student: Yeah, thanks for getting that. To be honest, I didn't know that me packing my bag early was so disruptive to you.

Teacher: You're surprised that bothers me.

Student: Yeah, I try to be quiet about it, but it seems to still bother you, and I guess I kind of get it since you're trying to wrap up the class and all.

Teacher: Thanks for understanding my point of view.

Student: Sure. I just don't know how to get to the other class on time if I don't pack my bag a minute before the bell rings.

Teacher: You're worried that it's just impossible for you to get to the other class on time.

Student: Yeah, and that teacher is super strict about us being on time.

Teacher: You don't want to disappoint and anger the other teacher.

Student: Right, when she gets mad, it's like world war three. But I also don't want to anger you.

Teacher: Sounds like you really don't want to upset anyone here.

Student: Yeah, I don't. Just don't know what to do.

Teacher: You're in a bind. Would you like some ideas?

Student: Do you have any?

Teacher: What if you commit to going straight to the other class without taking much time at all to talk to your friends on the way there? You can still say hi quickly but then continue on your way. And I'll write you a one-minute tardy slip just in case you are a couple of seconds or one minute late.

Student: I guess I'll try it and see.

Teacher: "Thanks, I really appreciate it. We can see how that works out and we can revisit it if this solution doesn't seem to work.

Student: Sounds good.

Note that while this interaction took a minute longer than the previous one, both student and teacher feel seen, and the problematic behavior is a lot less likely to occur again. Furthermore, the teacher doesn't have to spend additional time trying to calm down and regulate after a tumultuous exchange. Active listening saves a lot of time and energy.

Is Active Listening Coddling Students?

Some teachers may feel that active listening coddles students, that it absolves them of responsibility for their actions, and that a direct and commanding approach is more appropriate. These teachers forget four important things:

1. Active listening is to be used when students have problems, not all the time. If everything is going well, you can take a more assertive approach.
2. The whole point of active listening is for students to solve their own problems. It's the opposite of coddling them. It facilitates use of their prefrontal cortex and makes room for them to come up with effective solutions.
3. Students are humans, not machines. And when humans are in distress, they don't respond well to commands. Even if they do what you command them to, they will harbor resentment or beat themselves up, neither of which leads to effective learning and well-being.
4. Students can't learn academic subjects if they are not in a state to be able to learn.

Students can't learn academic subjects if they are not in a state to be able to learn.

There may be times when a student won't care how they are impacting you, or times when actively listening to a student, even for a long time, will not resolve an issue. While these tools might not work 100 percent of the time, if you keep using them, you'll eventually become more skilled and will likely see powerful results—including some right away. At the very least, active listening can show students that you respect them and validate their experience while reinforcing that their maladaptive behaviors or the strategies they use at home don't work in your classroom.

The last important subskill to apply here is to speak in chunks, not in pages. When you communicate with someone, especially when you are in conflict with them, it's important that you keep your I-messages short and name your inferences in chunks.[15] Leave space for the other person to take in what you are saying and to respond. People can only process a finite amount of information, and they may tune you out when you share too much all at once.

Sometimes problematic behaviors persist. This occurs because a need has not been met either for the student or the teacher. The key is to get the needs of both sides met, and that cannot be done by dictating to the student how they are supposed to behave. Instead, we need to use a collaborative problem-solving (CPS) approach with the student. I highly recommend you take a deep dive into this approach using the QR code or go to eqschools.com/resources.

Active listening and CPS allow you to connect before you correct. Students have a much greater likelihood of solving their own problems and greater willingness to meet your needs once they are heard, seen, and understood.

If our job as educators was only to teach students, that would be a dream come true for most of us. But between reading and responding to emails, participating in meetings, lesson planning, grading, and more, our plate gets filled fast. Sometimes we also have to deal with a difficult parent, which can become particularly draining. But if you have some effective communication tools to use with that parent, even they can become a fan of yours, and the conversation won't end up taking much of a toll.

Communicating with (Difficult) Parents

The vast majority of parents are reasonable and well-meaning people. Yet when it comes to their own kids, even reasonable people can become tricky. Here are communication strategies that can turn even an angry parent into a fan!

Before the Meeting

STEP 1: Get clear about the problem, the ways you can help, and the ways the parent can help.

- What is the observable problematic behavior that you can point to?
- Are there examples you can provide to concretize the problematic behavior?
- What are one or two strategies that you can commit to implementing to support the child?
- What are one or two strategies that the parent can use to support the child? Remember that the responsibility to help the child succeed lies with both you and the parent, not just you.

STEP 2: (This step is optional but recommended.) Review the Mastering Your Mindset for a Difficult Conversation with a Parent Mindset Guidelines. Get this resource with the QR code.

STEP 3: Review the pillars of attuned communication from earlier in this chapter.

STEP 4: Invite the parent to meet with you for twenty minutes, ideally in your department office—if there is a quiet and private space. If other people will be in the vicinity, the parent will be less likely to communicate poorly. If you must meet in your classroom, meet by the door and leave it slightly open.

STEP 5: If possible, invite the parent to bring the child with them to the meeting. (Less applicable in elementary school.) Most parents behave more reasonably in front of their children, and you will likely get to the issue at hand faster.

STEP 6: Ten minutes before the meeting, do the following three things:

- Spend one minute taking four rhythmic breaths. Breathe in to the count of four, hold your breath for a count of four, and breathe out to the count of eight. This will help you downregulate your nervous system.
- For one to two minutes, visualize yourself staying calm and collected no matter what happens in the meeting. What do you look like when you are calm? What does it feel like? Then visualize the meeting going better than you expected. Is the parent acknowledging you for something? Are they leaving with a smile?
- For two minutes, gather your thoughts and the points you'd like to make during the meeting.

During the Meeting

STEP 1: Sit by the parent's side and leave about two feet of space between you. Have a sample of the student's work on a chair or desk (or on your computer) in front of both of you. This will serve as a point of reference that you can both focus on, and it immediately sends a message that you are working together. Sitting face to face can feel adversarial, especially if there is a desk in between you.

STEP 2: Set context for the meeting. Start by welcoming them and thanking them for coming. Then share how the meeting is going to go. Tell them that after a quick check-in, you'll be happy to hear their questions or concerns, you will address them, and then you will share the points you want to make to see how you can work together to support their child.

STEP 3: Before you delve into concerns or questions, ask them how they are today. And give them some space to share.

STEP 4: Invite them to share their questions or concerns. At this stage it's important to note that difficult parents might very well shift away from talking about objective concerns. Instead of saying "My son earned a D on the last two tests and I'd love to learn how I might support him," the parent might attack you as a teacher: "Your grading is completely unreasonable and I've talked to other parents of kids in the class who think exactly the same thing." Your job at this point is to stay quiet, even though it's hard. Unless the parent is being blatantly disrespectful, yelling at you, or cussing you out, stay calm, stay quiet, and take in what they are saying. If they are blatantly disrespectful, say the following: "We cannot continue the meeting in this fashion. I'm going to leave now, and if you want to meet again, we're going to meet with my department head."

STEP 5: This is a powerful EQ Schools move that I call "the defuser." Assuming you didn't have to leave the meeting but that the parent did say things that were hard to hear, first acknowledge the parent for having the courage to tell you these things. You can say: "Thank you for sharing these things with me. I appreciate your courage and honesty, as most people don't share exactly what is on their mind." Most people who exhibit difficult behavior expect others to respond to them defensively, so when you acknowledge them instead, that immediately defuses them, and their nervous system begins to downregulate. The name of the game with people who behave in a difficult way is to defuse them first. If you don't, they will continue to fight and you will never get to the actual issue at hand.

STEP 6: After you acknowledge the parent, ask the following question: "Is there more?" This immediately lets them feel that you heard them and want to get the totality of their experience. They feel seen, and that helps regulate their system. And if there *is* more, it's better to lay it all out in the beginning. That way, you can address everything before resentment builds.

STEP 7: Describe what you hear them say and empathize with them. Use the pillars of attuned communication.

STEP 8: Once they finish, ask "Is there more?" again. If there is, repeat step 7. If they say no, move on to the next step.

STEP 9: This is another powerful EQ Schools move. If there is a sliver of truth to what the parent is saying, acknowledge it. It is rare for there to be zero truth in what a person is saying. Of course, if they tell you that you're a jerk, you leave the meeting. But if they tell you your grading is completely unreasonable, you can start by saying: "I get it. I have high expectations for my students, and sometimes it can feel intense to some students and some parents." By acknowledging a kernel of truth, you disarm the other person and show them that you are a reasonable human being. Again, it's all in the name of increasing the likelihood of regulating their nervous system so you can tackle the real issue at hand—their child's learning.

By acknowledging a kernel of truth, you disarm the other person.

STEP 10: Refocus the conversation on the real issue and reinforce collaboration by saying: "Thanks for sharing all of that with me. I deeply care about (child's name) and want to give them every opportunity to be successful in my class. I have some suggestions in mind about how *we* can help them. Would you like to hear them?" The last question is important because you are priming the parent's brain to listen. Wait for an aligned yes. If they say yes tentatively, you can ask: "Are you sure?" In most cases, they will want to hear your suggestions.

STEP 11: Provide the suggestions you thought of in step 1 of "Before the Meeting." For example: "Let's be sure your child comes to tutorial time so I can give them more one-on-one support." Or "Check in with your child on a daily basis about their homework progress." Only provide suggestions that you feel comfortable with. And I recommend including one or two things that the parent could easily do as well. If the parent asks you to do something that you are not sure you can commit to, let them know you'll need to think about it first. If you can't commit to the request, perhaps due to the number of students you have, you can share this decision but assure the parent that you are still committed to supporting their child together with them.

STEP 12: State the following: "Let's start with this plan and see whether that helps the situation. Hopefully it will, and if not, we can reconvene in the future to come up with another plan. How does that sound?" If they say they don't have much faith that it will work, first empathize with their feeling by saying something like: "I get how difficult it can be to not be certain if this plan will work." Then add: "It's important to start somewhere so we can provide your child with support right away." If the parent is still not sure, you can say that this is what you've come up with so far and that you might be able to think of other possibilities later on.

STEP 13: To close the meeting, gently let the parent know your next meeting is about to start: "Just so you know, I do have another meeting in a few minutes. I just want to assure you again that I'll do everything in my power to support your child, and I deeply appreciate you coming to meet with me today."

Remember that you may represent whatever school means to a parent based on their own childhood experiences (positive or negative). As much as possible, don't take things personally. Try to stay nonjudgmental and be compassionate.

Don't Try to Be Perfect and Don't Be Afraid to Apologize

Teachers are humans, and we juggle a lot every day. So it's understandable that even when we set out to be present, patient, enthusiastic, and engaging, we can easily become irritated, distracted, tired, angry, and short with students, colleagues, parents, and even our loved ones at home. Trust that you will be all these things throughout the year. None of us wants to lose it on a student, but if you do, follow these steps:

- Use the regulated breathing technique in the "Awareness" chapter for three breaths (it takes twenty seconds).
- Avoid beating yourself up and instead take a moment to be gentle with yourself, reminding yourself that you are human and you can't be perfect.
- Reflect on what caused you to feel triggered. Pinpoint the exact moment it happened and remember what you felt in your body.
- Consider what part of your body needs calmness. Invite that part to soften by taking a deep breath and mentally saying "soften" to it.
- Own your part in the interaction that caused distance or damaged the relationship.

- Take responsibility by naming your action explicitly to the student and apologizing for your behavior. And stop there. If you want to express your needs, save it for another time.

Since most adults never apologize to kids, taking responsibility and apologizing for your behavior can be shocking (in a good way) to your student and can go a long way toward repairing the relationship and modeling to the child that it's OK to apologize. It also increases the likelihood that they will apologize to you if they hurt, frustrate, or disrespect you in the future.

Since the most important relationship in your life is the one with yourself, you must remember to first treat yourself with care and compassion when adversity strikes. The beginning and ending of Rabbi Hillel's quote summarized this beautifully: "If I am not for myself, who will be for me? If I am only for myself, what am I? And if not now, when?" We'll delve into how to truly be there for ourselves in the next chapter.

> "If I am not for myself, who will be for me? If I am only for myself, what am I? And if not now, when?"
>
> —Rabbi Hillel

Journal Prompts to Enrich Your Relationships in Life and at Work

Here are questions to ask yourself about the state of your relationships. I highly recommend you pick the three that speak to you the most and that you answer them before continuing to read. Revisit this list once a quarter.

- What are three to five qualities that I love about my partner? (If you don't have a partner, choose your closest friend.) Do they notice my love language and provide it to me? Do they make me laugh? Do they have the capacity to be very present when they are with me? Does their touch feel amazing? Do I love having fun with them? Do they see me like no one else does? (List the qualities and write about how these qualities enrich your life. Then find a time to connect with your partner or friend, ideally in person, and tell them you had a moment of gratitude that they are in your life. Then ask if you could share a bit more with them. Share what you wrote and stay present for their reaction.)
- On a scale of 1 to 10, how satisfied am I in my relationship with my intimate partner? Is that number satisfactory to me? What does my response bring up for me?
- In what ways do I feel that my friends see me, understand me, want to know more about me? In what ways do I provide that to others?
- In what relationship do I laugh the most? What can I do to have 10 percent more time with that person than I currently do?
- Who do I rely on most for support? How easy or hard is it for me to rely on support from others? What will allow me to rely more on others?

- How do I show love in my relationship with my partner? With my kids? With my mother? With my father? With my siblings? With my best friend?
- What relationship do I have the most fun in? Why?
- Do I feel like my squad (the five people you hang out with the most) allows for me to fully express my potential? Are there any people I need to love from afar? Are there any people I want to draw more into my life?
- Is there anyone in my life who I need to forgive?
- Which people do I share my goals and dreams with? Who is most supportive of my goals?

Enrich Your Classroom with Playful Activities That Deepen Connections

Group/Partner Games

NAME GAME WITH GESTURES. Participants stand in a circle. Each person thinks of a small action that they can perform while saying their name. You can start by saying your name and doing an action, then have everyone repeat your name and do the action with you. For example, you'll say "Ms. Jones" and raise your arms up. Then everyone will say "Ms. Jones" and raise their arms up. You move on to the next person, and everyone repeats their name and gesture.

Once you've gone around the circle, the game can begin. Say your name and do your movement, then say someone else's name and do their movement. That will "pass" it to them. They will say their name and do their movement, then say someone else's name and do their movement to pass it to them. And the game continues.

Encourage people to help one another if they get stuck. A big lesson in this game is kindness and supporting one another. If the group is larger than twenty, break it into smaller groups.

For an instructional video of this game, use the QR code or go to eqschools.com/resources.

PASS THE BALL. Participants stand in a circle. One person pretends to hold a large ball in their hands. They make eye contact with someone across the circle and pass the imaginary ball to them. That person needs to pretend to catch the ball and then pass it to someone else. That person catches it and passes it to someone else, etc.

After a minute or two, have students make a high-pitched "boowoo" sound when they pass the ball. It's a funny sound that makes people giggle and is fun to do. Importantly, tell them to also make the boowoo sound when they receive the ball from someone else. So they say boowoo on the catch *and* on the pass. It's easy for people to forget to do it when they receive the ball, so you might need to remind them a few times.

After another minute, tell students to make whatever sound they think of (as long as it's appropriate) when they pass the ball. However, they need to remember to repeat the sound that is thrown at them when they catch the ball, and then they can throw the ball to someone else with their own sound.

PASS THE BALL IN PAIRS. This is the same game as Pass the Ball, but students will be in pairs. The ball will be passed faster, and it's important that students remember to mimic their partner's sound on the catch before making their own sound on the pass.

Don't forget to pair them up yourself. If teachers tell students to pair up, even if there is an even number of students, there is almost always a student who is chosen last, and that can very easily create a scar for that kid. The same applies to group work.

COHERENT STORY. Pair students and ask the overall group to give you a name of a man. Someone in the group might say John. Then ask them for the name of an animal that starts with the same letter that the man's name starts with. Someone in the group might say jaguar. Then ask them for an adjective that starts with j. Someone might say jumpy. Then tell the group that each pair will be telling a story about John the jumpy jaguar.

Have each pair decide who is partner A and who is partner B. Partner A will begin the story, and after about twenty-five seconds, you say "switch." Then partner B has to take over from where partner A left off. After about twenty seconds, say "switch" again, and partner A needs to take over the story. Keep alternating between the two with shorter and shorter intervals.

After about ninety seconds, tell them to pause. Explain that they are going to finish the story by alternating word for word and that they should start with the following sentence: "And ever since that day . . ." So partner A will say "and," partner B will say "ever," partner A will say "since," etc., until they finish the story.

Ask students if they felt a bit overwhelmed when their partner changed the trajectory of the story from what they envisioned. They will likely agree that it felt a bit jarring. Then remind students that this is what we are asked to do in life all the time. We are asked to work with others and build off their ideas, which requires social flexibility.

KNIFE AND FORK. Pair your students up, or if you feel like a safe space has been established in your classroom, you can ask your students to walk like robots for ten seconds. You should demonstrate what your robot walk looks like. At the end of ten seconds, say "freeze." Everyone should stop right away. Tell them to find a partner near them. If someone doesn't have a partner, help them find someone or be their partner.

Once the students are in pairs, tell them you are going to call out things and that in five seconds or less, without talking, they are to transform themselves into these things. It's helpful to demonstrate it first with a volunteer. Shout "knife and fork" and see your students turn into that. Then shout something else, like "salt and pepper," and wait until they turn into that. Be sure to tell students to look at other pairs as they turn into these things. You can have students give ideas as well.

GOLDEN GATE BRIDGE. This game is similar to Knife and Fork, but your students will be in groups of four and you will give them between ten and fifteen seconds to become what you call out. Here are some ideas of things to call out: *Titanic*, a plane, a car, the zoo, a house. Remember to tell them to do it without talking and to look at other groups once they are done. Then ask the entire group to turn into the Golden Gate Bridge without talking.

For more games, use the QR code or go to eqschools.com/resources.

Connection Rituals

TAKING ROLL WITH 1 TO 10. About a month into the school year (and after hopefully establishing a safe space), instead of having students say "present" or "here" when you take roll, have them give you a number between 1 and 10 to express how well they are feeling today. For example, you will say the name Tommy, and he might respond with 8. Then you'll call on Tina, and Tina might respond with 9. Then you'll call on Sue, and she might respond with 2. This tells you a couple of important things. First, you've created a safe enough place for Sue to admit that she feels like a 2 today. Second, if Sue says she's at a 2, then whenever the students engage in independent or group work, you will know to take a moment to check in with Sue. This will send a message to Sue that you care about her and that she's not alone. If you consistently do this, over time you will see that before you even reach out to Sue, another student (Tina) will check in on her. In addition to that, Tommy, who is sitting in the back, will observe that Tina is checking in on Sue. Empathy is being modeled to other students in the class without you doing anything but taking roll.

APPRECIATION SPIES. At the beginning of the week, assign each student another student to "spy on" for good qualities that they can appreciate about them. Have them write one or two appreciations on a piece of paper every day. At the end of the week, collect all the appreciation sheets and read them yourself first (I highly recommend that you do not skip this part, as some students can be mean or have a weird sense of what is an appreciation and what isn't). Then pass the sheets to the students who were appreciated and have them read their sheet. Students are often amazed by what others appreciate about them.

2X10. There is a lot of research to show that if a student knows even one adult in their life cares about them, their risk of engaging in maladaptive behavior drops drastically. Therefore, if you know that a student in your class is struggling emotionally, it can make a world of difference (and sometimes save a life) if you decide to check in with that student for two minutes every day for a period of ten days. If you feel like two minutes is too much, can you spend one minute with them? Can you spend even just thirty seconds with them? The key is to do it for ten days in a row consistently, because that sends a message to the child that they are on your radar and that they are not alone.

CIRCLE OF CONNECTIONS. To access this resource, use the QR code or go to eqschools.com/resources.

RELATIONSHIPS

FOR ACTIVITIES WITH STUDENTS GO TO PAGE 78

Use the pillars of attuned communication: drop in with presence, notice nonverbal cues, get curious, reflect back, empathize, and acknowledge. *(Page 25)*

Name your inference using the three-step method. *(Page 40)*

Respond to students' bids for attention. *(Page 47)*

Use active listening with students when they own the problem. *(Page 58)*

Send an I-message when you own the problem by using the three-step approach. *(Page 63)*

THREE

AWARENESS

EMBRACING WORK & LIFE'S REALITY WITH EASE AND DELIGHT

Awareness is the greatest agent for change.

—Eckhart Tolle

Activate Awareness, Savor Ordinary Moments, and Overcome Obstacles Peacefully

Let me ask you a question, and be honest with yourself as you answer it. How much time do you spend ruminating about the past or worrying about the future? If you are like most people, the answer is the vast majority of the time. You see, our brain naturally puts us in the past or in the future, yet when we are present we can fully live the life that is actually in front

Worrying about the future

Ruminating about the past

of us instead of being in a virtual reality in our heads. Thinking with a purpose is helpful. Unconscious or mindless thinking causes us to miss life experiences.

Many of us spend most of our time living life mindlessly.[1] We eat mindlessly, we drive mindlessly, we grade mindlessly (I've done it many times), we can even teach mindlessly, and many of us spend time with our loved ones mindlessly.

When my son was nine years old, he asked me to play Lego with him. Specifically, he wanted us to build a Stegosaurus out of Lego. I jumped at the opportunity to spend some quality time with him, but as soon as I sat on the carpet, my mind wandered to my next speaking engagement, the next flight I had to catch, and my next work call. My son looked up at me intensely, and to my shock he said, "Aba!" (which means dad in Hebrew). I said, "What?" and he pointed his fingers to the Lego and said, "Stegosaurus." He knew that I wasn't with him. My body was there, but I wasn't. If I have the opportunity to spend quality time with my children, I want to be fully there because the present is where life is lived.

The present is where life is lived.

Being aware involves noticing our five senses, noticing sensations in our body, and catching our brain when it's ruminating about the past, worrying about the future, or simply floating into a virtual reality that we invent in our minds. It allows us to savor our experiences and to be more resilient because we can notice what our nervous system needs if we are dysregulated.

How Does Awareness Tie into Effective Teaching?

Awareness allows you to make better decisions in the classroom because you can notice more about yourself and your students and have more information to work with. It allows you to attune to your students' energy and needs and respond to them with the appropriate energy. It also gives you another superpower that is crucial for teaching: the ability to create space between any stimulus and your response to it.

STIMULUS ⟵ AWARENESS ⟶ RESPONSE

Does this scenario sound familiar to you? It's the last hour of teaching for the day, students are tired, you are tired, and it's hot. You're in the midst of giving your students instructions for the next activity and two students cannot stop talking to each other. This distracts you and other students, so you ask the two students to be quiet. They are quiet for a moment, but as soon as you start giving the instructions again, they resume talking to each other and distracting others. You ask them to be quiet again, a little more emphatically now. They stop for a moment. And then, just like clockwork, they continue talking. At this point, it would be easy (and understandable) for you to lose your shit and yell at the students or say something regrettable. The students' talking is a stimulus that triggers you, and you snap.

In his book *Man's Search for Meaning*, Viktor Frankl wrote that there is always a space between any stimulus and our response to it.[2] And the more awareness we have about what is happening inside us, the more space we create between a stimulus and our response to it. That space gives us the ability and freedom to choose how much we let the stimulus impact us and how we respond to it.

Instead of losing your shit at the two students who keep disrupting you and others, you can notice the stimulus, take a slow breath to downregulate your nervous system, send them a clear I-message, and continue with the lesson.

We receive thousands of stimuli daily, most of which don't trigger us; however, some can easily do so. For example, how much do these things drive you crazy?

- When students raise their hands and you think they're going to say something insightful, but you call on them and they say, "May I go pee?"
- When students ask, "What are we doing?" as soon as you finish giving instructions
- Pencil tapping
- Too many meetings
- When a student turns in no assignments for the entire semester and then asks for extra credit
- Students sharpening pencils while you give instructions
- Students writing on their desks
- When a student says, "But my mom lets me!"
- No-name papers
- When parents text their kids during class
- When people just leave the copier jammed
- The Reply All button for emails
- Kids jumping up or packing their backpacks (with loud zippers) before the bell rings
- When you hear "Is this for a grade?" for the thirty-seventh time
- When kids put their head on the table and "fall asleep" or really fall asleep

Here are stimuli that are even bigger triggers for most of us:

- Getting a nasty email from a parent
- Having a difficult colleague roll their eyes at an idea you provide in a PLC meeting

- Having your spouse or partner criticize your character
- Having your spouse or partner get defensive
- Financial worries (whether real or imagined)
- Worries about your health or the health of a loved one
- Your own children communicating contemptuously with you or their siblings (a teenager specialty)

What happens in our brain when a stimulus triggers us? When external stimuli trigger us, our hypothalamic-pituitary-adrenal axis, located in our limbic system (the emotional reasoning part of the brain), starts a process of self-protection that activates our sympathetic nervous system and leads us to behave in one of three ways: fight, flight, or freeze.[3] We experience a spike in stress hormones such as cortisol and adrenaline, which leads us to feel hijacked by our emotions, and we're unable to engage our healthy coping skills. Instead, we yell, fight, run away, stonewall, etc. The following true story illustrates beautifully how I got hijacked by my emotions during class. I'm not proud of it, but hey, I also don't want you to think I'm a perfect teacher. I'm not even close. I've just learned to be OK with that over time.

Daniel's Story

It was a beautiful April morning, and after five minutes of direct instructions, my E period AP Economics students were all hard at work, fully focused on the AP test review packet I'd given them. All except for Daniel, who, sure enough, was looking down at his phone underneath his desk.

This was not the first time I'd caught Daniel on his phone, and this time I lost my shit. I yelled at him to give me his phone and told him to start focusing like the rest of the students in the class or else I was going to kick him out altogether and keep his phone for a week. (Not that I could actually do that, but I was definitely not thinking using my pre-frontal cortex here. I was emotionally hijacked and in full fight mode.)

After class was dismissed, I had a prep period in which I couldn't stop ruminating over Daniel doing this in *my* class! Such disrespectful behavior! These thoughts kept on looping, so I decided to journal about the incident in the hope that I could clear my head and get productive. As I was journaling, I started to recognize that there was something deeper at play here because all my thoughts boiled down to "How could Daniel do this to me?" I was a victim and Daniel was the perpetrator. That's when the uh-oh rang through my head: I realized I'd taken it way too personally, had made it about myself, and had lost my shit needlessly.

I decided that instead of beating myself up about it, I would take a deep breath and use a self-compassion practice to regulate. In my practice, I had a powerful realization: the reason I lost it on Daniel was because I mindlessly fell into a trance of thoughts that my inner critic (what I affectionately call my gremlin or my itty bitty shitty committee) was feeding me.

It all happened fast. As soon as I noticed Daniel looking at his cell phone, my inner critic told me: "See, you're not that great a teacher after all, are you? They let you teach AP Economics and this is what happens—your students get on their cell phones. Why do they even let you teach at all? Your lessons are so boring!" It took about two seconds for me to feel angry, but more importantly, underneath the anger I felt shame because I bought into the false story that my inner critic was feeding me.

I felt the shame so strongly that I couldn't bear it anymore, so I employed a common strategy that adults and kids unfortunately use all the time. Instead of regulating my shame, I decided to shame Daniel. It was the fastest way for me to deal with that emotion, at least temporarily. Of course, the shame came back twofold, and I also damaged my relationship with Daniel.

While practicing self-compassion, I was able to see what happened objectively, and I could nonjudgmentally accept that my behavior fell short because I had a false belief about myself. It helped me recognize that I'd personalized the situation and that it was time for me to attempt a repair. I promised myself that when I met with Daniel, I would not only apologize for the way I reacted but also get curious (not judgmental) about why it's so hard for him to stay off his phone. Then I would use that information to start a collaborative problem-solving session with him so that we could, hopefully, put an end to this cell phone business.

I met with him the next day during lunch and started the conversation by saying: "Daniel, I wanted to chat about what happened yesterday in class. It wasn't OK that you were on your cell phone in class, and the way I reacted was not OK, either, and I'm sorry for that." Daniel was speechless and somewhat shocked. I learned later that no adult had ever apologized to him in his life, so he was just waiting for another lecture from me about how disrespectful he was. When all he got was a genuine apology, he thanked me and apologized for being on his cell phone.

I told him that I'd really like to understand why it's difficult for him to stay away from his cell phone. I made a point of telling him that my question was not coming from a place of negative judgment but from a place of care and genuine curiosity. His first answer was "I don't know," typical of a high school boy. I said, "No problem, take some time to think about it." After a few moments, he told me, "Mr. Habib, I think I'm addicted to my phone." I wanted to yell "No shit!" but I contained myself, and I was happy that the kid came to that realization himself. He also told me that one of his friends was suicidal and the Facebook profile he was refreshing every other second was hers. That turned out to be true, and because of our conversation, that student ended up getting the support she needed.

I asked Daniel if he would be willing to go through a collaborative problem-solving process with me to find a possible solution to this problem. After a few bad ideas, Daniel said, "What if every time I come to class, I put my phone on your desk in the beginning and pick it up at the end?" My mind exploded with joy and excitement. I couldn't believe that he would voluntarily let go of his phone for an hour—and more importantly that *he* came up with the solution!

Notice that what allowed me to become aware was journaling. Journaling is a powerful awareness tool, and it allowed me to then use a self-regulation tool (self-compassion), then relationship management tools (making a repair attempt and collaborative problem solving), and then a social awareness tool (approaching with curiosity). All these tools are emotional intelligence tools, and awareness is the foundation for them all. Notice also that if I'd had enough self-awareness in the first place, I could have handled the situation much more effectively from the beginning and saved myself (and Daniel) a lot of time and energy.

EQ SKILLS

JOURNALING
(SELF-AWARENESS)

SELF-COMPASSION PRACTICE
(SELF-REGULATION)

REPAIR ATTEMPT AND CPS
(RELATIONSHIP MANAGEMENT)

APPROACHING WITH CURIOSITY
(SOCIAL AWARENESS)

Managing Stress through Awareness

Stress is made up of two elements: the objective reality we face and the way we interpret that reality.

The bad news is that we cannot change number one. The good news is that the second element is a lot more predictive of how resilient we will be in the face of adversity. With more awareness, we can transform our interpretation of the reality that we face, our self-image, and our self-talk.

For us to make meaning of factual events in our lives, we co-create our reality by inventing and telling ourselves stories called counter-facts.[4] These counter-facts are a huge predictor of how happy and resilient we will be.

> We co-create our reality by inventing and telling ourselves stories called counter-facts.

The following example will make this concept more concrete. You get into your car to go to the grocery store. As you reach a busy intersection, your lane has a green light to turn left. Fifteen cars ahead of you turn left. When it's your turn to turn left, the light is still green. Right as you cross the intersection, a drunk driver runs a red light and ends up hitting your car straight on. Shaken up, you get out of your car, realizing that your left arm is badly wounded. Without thinking about it too much, do you consider yourself lucky or unlucky? What's the first response that comes to your mind?

Understand that in the process of answering this question, your brain is inventing a story that complements the objective facts. If you consider yourself lucky, your invented counter-fact is "I could have easily died. Thank goodness I'm alive!" If you consider yourself unlucky, your invented counter-fact is "I was totally healthy when I got in the car and now I'm injured!" Maybe you even say to yourself: "Out of all the cars on the road, I'm the one who got hit? That's horrible luck!" Your story is invented in milliseconds, and it is what determines your resilience and your well-being at that moment. We invent hundreds of these counter-facts every day, and the more awareness we have about how we interpret and co-create our reality, the more choice we have about how to respond to factual events.

> The more awareness we have about how we interpret and co-create our reality, the more choice we have about how to respond to factual events.

What's most important here is to understand that the choice is yours. You can consider yourself lucky if (and it's a big if) you are aware that you are inventing a story that shapes your experience.

Most of us spend a disproportionate amount of time worrying, ruminating, and obsessing about thoughts that are either completely false or mostly false, and these thoughts are completely out of our control and not worth spending our time and energy on in the first place.

The thoughts that make up our own self-judgment can be particularly vicious. Many of the educators I coached and trained believed these erroneous thoughts:

- I'm not an effective teacher.
- I'm not inspiring enough.
- People (my students, my colleagues, my supervisor) will think I'm a fraud.
- All my colleagues are working harder than me.
- I don't have what it takes to (fill in the blank).
- Teaching is too difficult and stressful for me.

- I can't support my students in the way that I should.
- I'm not a good enough mother/father.
- I'm not a good enough son/daughter.
- I'm not a good enough brother/sister.

Notice that all these thoughts can be classified as all-or-nothing thinking. I'm either an effective teacher or I'm not. I can either support my students or I can't. When we are stressed, we often resort to this type of thinking, yet it leads us to believe in what psychologists call cognitive distortions—thoughts that distort our reality. American psychiatrist David Burns came up with a list of the most common cognitive distortions that we engage in.[5] For the full list of cognitive distortions and strategies for reframing them, use the QR code or go to eqschools.com/resources.

If we were to look at our life or our work performance more realistically, we would see that we're not a complete failure and we're also not perfect. As teachers, we might not have the ideal tools to help all our students, but we can certainly help some. In other words, we live in shades of gray, not in a black-or-white world.

We live in shades of gray, not in a black-or-white world.

So how can we become more aware of what's going on within and around us instead of reacting to external stimuli or getting lost in a virtual reality? The most effective strategy is to regularly tend to our attention and notice what is happening within our body. That's where mindfulness comes in.

Attain Balance: Mindfulness for Smoother School Days and Beyond

According to Jon Kabat-Zinn, the creator of the Mindfulness-Based Stress Reduction (MBSR) program and one of the pioneers who brought mindfulness practices to the West, mindfulness is "paying attention in a particular way: on purpose, in the present moment, and non-judgmentally.[6]

"Tara Brach, psychologist, author of many books on the topic, and gifted mindfulness teacher, says that mindfulness is "a quality of awareness that recognizes exactly what is happening in our moment-to-moment experience."[7] And that it "allows us to see life as it is."[8]

And according to Harvard psychology professor Ellen Langer, who has devoted her career to the topic, mindfulness is "the simple act of actively noticing things."[9]

Many people equate mindfulness with meditation and think that you can only be mindful when you sit on a cushion with your eyes closed. As you can see from the definitions above, mindfulness is a quality that we can bring to anything we do. Right before your students walk into the classroom, you can decide that you are going to notice them and pay attention without judgment. When you are about to eat your sandwich, you can decide to pay attention to the wonderful taste of the food. When you wait in line at the store, you can notice the cashiers and the people around you without judgment. And if you feel impatient or annoyed by how slowly the line is moving, you can bring your attention to that in a gentle and compassionate way. Every time you walk outside in your neighborhood, you can decide to notice the trees, flowers, and people. Every time you notice you are dysregulated, you can take some mindful breaths.

> Mindfulness is a quality
> that we can bring to
> anything we do.

Mindfulness practice is the intentional act of training our mind to stay focused and our body to stay relaxed. The point of mindfulness practice is not to become more peaceful; that is a nice by-product of the practice. The point is that it is a practice. We are training our brain to be focused and relaxed so that it can be the same when we are not meditating. Over time, that translates to meeting our difficult students with more patience, understanding a controversial decision the district office has made (not necessarily agreeing with it), and being gentle with ourselves when we make mistakes.

When and Where to Practice: Create an Implementation Intention

To build a mindfulness practice into your life, schedule the practice for once a day, ideally at the same time, and practice in a room that gives you some privacy and is relatively soundproof.

To maximize the likelihood that you will actually practice, I highly recommend you create what psychologists call an implementation intention.[10] An implementation intention is a simple statement: "I will (activity) at (time of day) in (location) (frequency) for (duration)." For example: "I will practice at 7:00 a.m. on my couch daily for three weeks." Or if you want to make it even more simple: "I will (activity) at (time of day)." For example: "I will practice at 7:00 a.m." Write your implementation intention in a journal. The act of writing it will increase the likelihood that you will do it.

Mindfulness Practice Posture for Seated Practices

Practice on a chair or on a cushion. If you sit on a chair, get into a comfortable position sitting upright and relax your shoulders just a bit. Feel both of your feet firmly planted on the floor and place the palms of your hands on your lap facing up or down. Imagine that there is a string attached to the top of your head and it pulls you upright just a bit more, like a puppet being pulled by its string. If you sit on a cushion, sit cross-legged and ensure that your back is straight as you gaze forward. You may want to lean very slightly against a wall to support your position. Once you have established proper posture, gaze forward and see if anything else in your body wants to let go and relax a bit more. Perhaps your jaw can loosen a bit, or maybe your throat can soften. Just notice if there is any tension that wants to ease. Then you can close your eyes and begin your practice.

Focus, Relaxation, and Acceptance

In any mindfulness practice, there are three qualities you'll want to cultivate: focus, relaxation, and acceptance. Focus on the anchor you've chosen (whether it's your breath, a body part, a sound, or something else) and keep that anchor in your awareness with specific, sustained attention. Couple this focus with relaxation. Every time you exhale, let your body soften and relax while you remain focused on your anchor. This relaxation will allow you to accept whatever arises in you during the practice with gentleness. You may notice it's hard to concentrate or that sadness comes up. Perhaps your stomach is churning or a thought makes you smile. You can practice nonjudgmentally accepting that whatever is here is here, and you can patiently come back to your anchor.

Specific Mindfulness Practices That I Love and Recommend

There are many different types of mindfulness practices, and I'm not going to list them all. Instead, I've categorized them into two main groups, and I've listed the ones that I believe are most impactful. Closed-focus practices bring our focus inward and help us attune to what is happening within us moment to moment. Open-focus practices allow us to sharpen our senses and attune more deeply to our surroundings.

I encourage you to start each practice by silently repeating the words of Randee Schwartz, a gifted RYT 500 yoga instructor: "In the next few moments, there is nothing for me to do, nowhere for me to go, and no one for me to be." And at the end of each practice, say to yourself: "May I come back to my body as I am, in this moment as it is. Return to my body with gentle movement and return to my mind with loving thoughts."

Closed-Focus Mindfulness Practices: Somatic Awareness

Gut Awareness

(One minute to ten minutes.) Find yourself in a mindful body posture, and if you are not too tired, close your eyes. Otherwise keep your eyes half open and gaze at the floor. Then place one hand on your stomach and use your full awareness to notice how your gut feels as it expands with each inhalation and contracts with each exhalation. Keeping your hand on your stomach, breathe normally at first and then slowly begin to slow your breath (slow the exhalation even more than the inhalation). Once your breath has slowed some, bring your awareness to your gut again. Notice any movement or energy you're feeling. Invite that region of your body to soften with every exhalation.

Regulated Breathing

(One to three minutes.) This practice allows us to downregulate our nervous system. Find yourself in a mindful body posture. Take ten regulated breaths by inhaling to the count of four, holding for four, and exhaling to the count of eight. Inhale, two, three, four. Hold, two, three, four. And exhale, two, three, four, five, six, seven, eight. Slow your breath progressively, and after ten breaths allow your breath to return to its natural speed. With each breath, allow yourself to feel more and more still. Remember that if thoughts come to you, you must allow them to pass as soon as you're aware that you're no longer focused on your breath. Do so gently and nonjudgmentally for the next few moments.

Closed-Focus Mindfulness Practices: Cognitive Awareness

Focused Breathing and Noticing Thoughts

(Three minutes to twenty-five minutes.) Find yourself seated in a mindful body posture in a room with few or no distractions. Close your eyes and bring your awareness to your breath at the opening of your nostrils above your upper lip. Sense the breath in this region. You can notice the difference between how cool the air is when you inhale and how warm it is when you exhale. Or simply notice how your nostrils feel as the air goes in and out.

Invariably, thoughts will enter your mind, and you will not be aware right away that your attention is no longer on your breath. That is a perfectly fine and natural part of the practice. The intention with this practice is to catch yourself no longer noticing your breath as soon as you can, and when you do, to congratulate yourself for having a mindful moment. Then, gently and nonjudgmentally redirect yourself to sensing your breath.

Some days it will be easier to remain focused on your breath, and other days it will be harder. This process of gently bringing our attention back can happen tens or hundreds of times in a practice. Even if you spend eight minutes of a ten-minute practice lost in thoughts, be gentle with yourself as you come back to your breath. Remember that there is no competition here, and the aim is not to be perfect. It is simply to practice and cultivate the capacity to focus and stay relaxed at the same time. As we do this, we change our neural pathways. We increase our capacity to catch our thoughts when we're off the cushion and to decide whether we want to choose these thoughts or more empowering and helpful thoughts. It may be helpful for you to set a timer that rings a gong every five minutes to remind you to bring your awareness back to your breath.

Body Scan

(Five minutes to fifteen minutes.) Use the QR code or go to eqschools.com/resources to access this resource.

Noting

(Three minutes to twelve minutes.) Use the QR code or go to eqschools.com/resources to access this resource.

Closed-Focus Mindfulness Practices: Self-Compassion

(Eight minutes to twenty-five minutes.) This practice was adapted from a practice that Kristen Neff, a leading researcher on self-compassion, teaches.[11] It helps us resource ourselves and become our best coach. Consider using the resourcing script on page 120 to create a safe place for yourself before delving into this exercise.

When you are ready, bring to mind something that is causing you suffering or stress. This can be in relation to another person, or it can be a general sense of worry or anxiety. Let any emotion that arises just be. Whether it's shame, fear, guilt, or anger, allow that emotion to stay, and for the next few breaths, repeat in your mind: "This is hard" or "This is tough" or "This hurts."

Then bring your hand to your heart and touch your heart with an intentionally soothing touch. See if you can bring a quality of warmth to your touch with the next few breaths, and invite your heart to relax and ease just a bit more.

Next, bring to mind what you look like when you are calm, relaxed, and in your "adult" self. With the vision of your adult self, silently repeat the following phrases of intentional kindness: "Sweetie, this is hard, and I'm here for you. You are not alone. I'm not leaving you. I'm by your side, and we're going to get through this together. There is nothing wrong with feeling what you are feeling. Everyone suffers. I'm not leaving. And I love you. Not for what you accomplish or for what you do but simply because you exist."

Continue to breathe in and out deeply, repeating these sentences to yourself for the next few minutes. If emotions or tears come up, let them come up and allow yourself to feel fully and love yourself fully. If at any point it feels like too much (which can often happen with self-compassion—it's a phenomenon called backdraft), visualize yourself back in your nourishing place, safe and supported.

When you are ready, ask yourself: "What else do I need to tell myself now as I slowly come out of the practice?" Some options are: "May I continue to be kind to myself throughout today" or "It's OK for me to feel what I feel" or "I can ask for help." Take a few deep breaths, repeating that statement several times. Then take a few more breaths and visualize yourself in your nourishing place thanking your "adult" self for showing up for you when most needed. Slowly open your eyes, allowing yourself to come back into the physical room, and take three mindful breaths before proceeding with your day.

An important note on self-compassion: Some people hear the words self-compassion and roll their eyes as if to say "I'm not built for this soft, mooshy stuff." What they don't realize is that this soft, mooshy stuff is exactly what we need when we face the toughest tests in our lives. It's what allows us to move through a divorce, through getting fired, through losing a loved one, through a difficult tantrum by our two-year-old (or teenager), or through a difficult fight with our partner. It's what allows us to continue to take risks as an educator even when we fail and are afraid to try again. It's what allows us to learn from our mistakes and to lead and teach courageously.

These practices provide us with a baseline of security that most people crave and do not have. It's the ultimate sense of being held and it's independent of anyone else. Nothing can shake it. It's unflappable. You can always lean on that whenever you experience adversity, and the world doesn't seem nearly as scary. You can be your own most nourishing parent and your own place of safety.

For a deeper understanding of the self-compassion mindfulness practice, use the QR code or go to eqschools.com/resources.

Open-Focus Mindfulness Practices: Loving Kindness

(Five minutes to twenty minutes.) Find yourself seated in a mindful body posture in a room with few or no distractions. Close your eyes and bring your awareness to your breath, taking three deep breaths. Now imagine that you are surrounded by three people: a person you love, a person you don't know very well, and a person you sometimes find difficult but who you feel safe with. Turn to the first person, and with the next breath, silently say "May you be happy." Imagine them happy and maybe even laughing. Then, with the next breath, say "May you be healthy." Imagine them strong, flexible, and well. And finally, say "May you be at peace." See them feeling calm and relaxed with not a worry on their mind.

Repeat the same process with your acquaintance and the person in your life who feels difficult. It's usually harder to do this with the acquaintance and the difficult person, yet if we can cultivate loving kindness for those we usually don't think about or those who challenge us the most, it begins to shift our behavior and attitude toward others in powerful ways in our day-to-day life. Taking the step from sending love to people who are close to us to those who aren't is huge when it comes to cultivating compassion.

Finally, take some time to send these messages to yourself: "May I be happy," "May I be healthy," and "May I be at peace." As you breathe, really take the time to visualize what you look like when you're happy, laughing, and content. How does it feel internally to be energetic, healthy, and strong? What do you look like when you are calm and have no worries on your mind? Take some deep breaths with these visualizations in your mind and heart. You can then send love to all beings in the universe by repeating: "May all beings be happy, may all beings be healthy, may all beings be at peace." When you're ready, slowly open your eyes.

I often end my focused breath mindfulness practices with a heartfulness practice that is aimed at setting my intentions for the day. If I care about being focused and gentle with myself, I silently repeat: "May I be focused. May I be gentle with myself." I visualize what it feels like to be focused and gentle with myself as well as what I look like when I'm in those states.

Open-Focus Mindfulness Practices: Mindful Touch/Taste

(One minute to five minutes.) Mindful touch and taste practices connect the outside world with our internal somatic experience. Have you ever eaten one raisin or one grape slowly enough to fully take in all the different textures and tastes that come along with that experience? It's amazing how much we miss by rushing. These practices allow us to experience more of the simple joys of the world, whether it's the taste of food or the way the sun feels on our skin on a warm day.

Open-Focus Mindfulness Practices: Mindful Listening

(One minute to ten minutes.) Use the QR code or go to eqschools.com/resources to access this resource.

Open-Focus Mindfulness Practices: Mindful Seeing

(One minute to ten minutes.) Use the QR code or go to eqschools.com/resources to access this resource.

How Long Do I Have to Practice to See Long-Term, Positive Effects?

The amount of time should sufficiently challenge you, but it should not leave you frustrated or demoralized. Similar to physical exercise, you should build a greater and greater capacity to do the practice. No one should run five miles without having run a day in their life before. And you shouldn't try to meditate for one hour if you've never done it before either. I recommend starting with a five-minute practice and working up to at least twelve minutes per day.

Consistency

A more important question than how long you should practice is how often you should practice. The answer is once or twice daily, and the more consistent you are, the faster you will see results. I've been meditating for two decades using various methods, from vipassana meditation to yoga, and while I have certainly skipped some days, I've done everything in my power to not skip more than one day at a time. Meditating consistently has been transformational for me.

It is not willpower that allows me to stay consistent. I use tricks that I've successfully applied to other habits, such as working out. Here are six tools that help tremendously with consistency:

- **Do a short practice rather than no practice at all.** If you find that you only have two minutes to practice, it's much better for you to do that than to skip the practice. This keeps the momentum of the routine of the practice.

- **Find an accountability buddy.** Three years ago, I made a pact with a friend that we would text each other every time we finished our meditation. I committed to practicing every day, and knowing that my friend would be waiting for my text motivated me to prioritize my practice over other pressing items on my to-do list.

- **Mark your calendar.** Buy a physical calendar that you can place on a wall. Every day that you meditate, draw a small dot. The visual cue of the completed meditation is very satisfying and reinforces your desire to draw another dot on the next day. Many people find that once a few dots are up, they don't want to break the chain, which provides additional motivation to stay consistent.

- **Don't beat yourself up if you miss a day.** Remember that a key to mindfulness practice is that when we notice we're not focused on our anchor (whether it's the breath, the body, a sound, or an object), we want to come back to it with gentleness, compassion, and patience. If you miss a day, approach this with gentle acceptance. It will allow you to start up again much faster.

- **Don't miss two days in a row.** Missing one day is an anomaly. Missing two days in a row is the beginning of a trend. Try to avoid that as much as possible, but if you do miss two days in a row, don't beat yourself up. With gentleness, recommit to the practice and do it.

- **Use an app such as Calm, Headspace, or Ten Percent Happier.** You certainly do not need one to stay consistent, but an app can send you a reminder to practice, it can show you a calendar of your practices, and it has many guided practices that can help you stay on track.

Awareness Coupled with Acceptance: 4 Ns Strategy

When we face adversity or are triggered by difficult people, awareness coupled with a deep sense of acceptance can be particularly powerful. This can be acceptance of ourselves and of whatever we are currently experiencing.

The 4 Ns strategy below incorporates awareness, self-regulation, and self-compassion. You can use it quickly (in as little as one minute) and still get benefits from it.

Step 1: Notice the Signs Your Body Gives You

When we're triggered, the simple act of noticing the signals of our body sets the foundation that allows us to depart from our fight, flight, or freeze mode. The internal process we experience when we receive a nasty email from a colleague, get rejected for a promotion, notice a contemptuous look from our partner, or have to deal with a student who is yelling in class is similar to what we experience when we are in actual imminent physical danger—even though our brain can distinguish the difference after a few moments. Whether the stimulus triggers anxiety, trauma, or anger, our sympathetic nervous system sends hormones that increase our alertness, our heart rate, our breathing rate, and even the amount of glucose in our bloodstream. Our body is sending us a clear message that says: "Pay attention to me!"

While it is common to feel hijacked by our body's reaction to the stimulus, it is possible, a split second later, to tell yourself: "Wow, I just felt hijacked. My body just told me that. I'm noticing it in my heart, chest, and throat."

Setting the intention to notice your body signals when triggered will help you notice them fast, and the more you practice, the easier it will become. Also, daily mindfulness somatic practice will help you be more attuned to those signals.

Step 2: Name What You Are Experiencing

Every emotion is tied to a sensation in our body.[12] The word *emotion* comes from the Latin root *emovere*, which means energy in motion. When we experience an emotion, we experience energy moving in our body. That is why emotions are often referred to as feelings—because we can literally feel the sensation of the emotion in our body. If you want to read about a research study that proves this, use the QR code or go to eqschools.com/resources to access this resource.

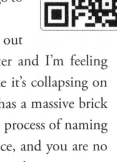

Name the sensation and emotion silently (or out loud) to yourself: "Wow, my heart is beating faster and I'm feeling angry!" or "Whoa, my chest feels so heavy and like it's collapsing on itself, I'm scared" or "Ah, my stomach feels like it has a massive brick in it because I'm just feeling so sad about this." The process of naming what is going on immediately tames your experience, and you are no longer hijacked by the emotion and sensation. Instead, you are now an observer of the emotion and sensation, and you can approach your experience with equanimity (mental calmness). As Dr. Daniel Siegel says, whatever you name, you tame.[13]

If you're having a hard time noticing where you feel your emotions in your body, you can simply notice your heart either by putting a hand on it or by bringing your awareness to your chest and naming whatever emotions you experience.

Whatever you name,
you tame.

Step 3: Normalize Your Emotions

The only dangerous emotion is a repressed emotion—whatever you resist persists. If you try to stuff an emotion down, it will become stronger over time and take more of your energy. You are experiencing these emotions because you are human. There are two groups of people in the world who don't feel difficult emotions: psychopaths and dead people. So if you are experiencing emotions such as anger, shame, and fear, that's a great sign. In other words, there is nothing wrong with you.

Give yourself the permission to be human by allowing the feelings to be there. I recommend that you even silently tell yourself: "I'm feeling angry with this kid, and it makes sense that I am; I'm human, and most people would feel the same" or "I'm feeling ashamed of making this mistake in front of my colleagues; most people would feel exactly the same way" or "I'm feeling afraid because I'm human; there is nothing wrong with me." To be clear, you are not justifying any bad behavior on your part, and you are not asserting that you have a right to feel like this forever. You are simply saying: "At this moment, I'm feeling (emotion), and that is OK." This step is our bridge from the sympathetic nervous system (fight, flight, or freeze) to the parasympathetic nervous system, the rest-and-digest mode of our nervous system.

Step 4: Nurture Yourself

This last step allows us to fully activate our parasympathetic nervous system so we can experience a physiological shift and a rush of soothing hormones such as serotonin and endorphins. The fastest and most effective way to do this is by stimulating our vagus nerve (the longest nerve in our body, which connects our gut, heart, and brain).[14] The easiest way to stimulate the vagus nerve is through the regulated breathing exercise on page 99. The longer exhalations activate vagal tones in our body, which allows the parasympathetic nervous system to take hold. If you only have time to take a couple of deep breaths before you respond

The only dangerous emotion is a repressed emotion— whatever you resist persists.

to a stimulus, those breaths can make all the difference between having a rotten rest of the day or an amazing rest of the day.

You can deepen the nurturing and soothing experience by using one or two hands to touch the part of your body that is feeling most active. Use intentional warmth and compassion. This allows us to bypass our thinking brain and to experience, at the deepest level, that we are cared for and that we are safe. With every exhalation, invite that part of your body to soften by silently saying the word *soften* and visualizing that part of the body relaxing.

Finally, you can use the self-compassion practice from page 100 to soothe the difficult emotion that you're experiencing. "I see you, shame, and it's OK for you to stay here. We're going to move through this together."

Another powerful nurturing practice is called the Quick Coherence Technique.[15] It was developed by Doc Childre at the HeartMath Institute. Use the QR code or go to eqschools.com/resources to access this resource.

While we have a varying amount of time to react to different triggers, you can apply different parts of the 4 Ns in any circumstance. For example, if you need to respond to a student right away because they are being very disruptive in class, you can take one regulated breath to immediately downregulate your nervous system. If you receive a nasty email from a parent but have to start teaching right away, you can go through the noticing and naming steps and take one deep breath. Then at the end of the day, before replying to the email, you can take five minutes to go through the full 4 Ns process.

By applying the 4 Ns, we can shift our biology. This emotional-regulation strategy can lead the shape of curve of our heart rate variability to become smoother, indicating greater heart coherence, and with that comes a shift in our mood.

It is often tempting to solve problems right away, when we're still in a frustrated or disempowered state. But it's much more fruitful to put ourselves in a regulated, coherent, and empowered state before working to solve problems. This will allow us to come up with much more effective and creative solutions. Emotional awareness makes us more intelligent.

Journal Prompts to Deepen Awareness in Your Life

Below is a freewrite prompt and some questions to ask yourself that will deepen your awareness:

- Freewrite for five minutes without stopping. Write about whatever comes to your mind and don't worry about spelling or grammar. Simply allow your thoughts to go on the page, and if you feel stuck, write "I feel stuck and I don't know what to write about" as many times as you need until you naturally feel unstuck.

- What thought is preoccupying my mind now? Is that thought true? Can I know with 100 percent certainty that it's true? How do I feel and behave when I believe that thought? How would I feel if I couldn't think that thought? (Adopted from Byron Katie's questions in *Loving What Is*.[16])

- What made me smile today? How did I feel in my body at that moment? How can I have more of that in my life?

- What story am I telling myself right now? Is it helpful? Is it true? If not, what is the more accurate story?

- In the last two hours, how present was I in my experience and with those around me?

- What is the strongest emotion that I'm experiencing right now? Where do I feel it in my body?

- When am I going to slow down today to notice how I feel? And how will I do it?

- What will I do today if I feel stressed or anxious?

- How is my body feeling now?

- How am I going to make today a great day?

- How did I move through challenges today? What can I acknowledge myself for?

- How can I approach tomorrow with ease and curiosity?

How I Cultivated Mindfulness Practices with Students

Happiness does not depend on what you have or who you are. It solely relies on what you think.

—Buddha

I almost didn't implement mindfulness practices in my classroom at all because I had three main fears. The first was that students would hate it. They would think it's lame and that I was trying too hard to create a kumbaya environment. The second was that parents would sue me because they'd think I was initiating their children into a cult. You have to understand that while the vast majority of parents in Palo Alto are sane and very supportive of teachers, as in any city, there are a few that are pretty nuts. One parent once called me a Nazi (I'm Jewish, by the way) because he felt that my grading rubric was too harsh and that his child, despite not trying at all in my class, should pass. And Palo Alto's crazy parents have the means to hire crazy lawyers, so inviting their children into mindfulness practices was not necessarily risk free. The third thing I feared was losing instructional minutes. I was teaching AP Economics at the time, which covered a ton of material, and I needed all the time I could get.

I shared these fears with one of my colleagues and asked him whether I was about to develop a reputation for being this weird, tree-hugging, peyote-smoking hippie teacher who believed in peace and love more than academic rigor. He gave me one of the best pieces of advice I've ever gotten. He said, "Roni, you are not that important. No teacher or student will be lying in bed at two a.m. thinking to themselves, 'That Mr. Habib . . . he's a kumbaya hippie, man.' People are busy with their own lives and they don't think about you that much. Go for it!"

I decided that I was going to give these strategies a shot for one week. If it all went well, I would continue for one more week. If it bombed, well, I would acknowledge myself for taking a risk even if it was scary by celebrating my failure with a "Woohoo!"

Here's what happened.

To my surprise, the mindfulness practices were a big hit with the vast majority of my students. I didn't fully understand why they liked them so much until I decided to shadow one of my students for the day. Shadowing a student means that you follow them wherever they go for the entire day. This was one of the most powerful empathy-building exercises I've ever experienced. For a detailed description of that experience, use the QR code or go to eqschools.com/resources to access this resource.

The biggest aha moment for me was this: we are teaching our kids to be human doings, not human beings.

We are teaching our kids to be human doings, not human beings.

My students enjoyed the mindfulness practices not only because of what they learned about themselves, but also because this was the only time during their frantically fast-paced day when they had a moment of peace. They got to experience a moment in which they could connect to their bodies and notice how they were actually doing. They experienced a moment of letting go of their future worries and ruminations about the past, and they didn't have to uphold any persona like so many students (and adults) do. They could simply be. At the end of the practices, I found them to be much calmer, and after a few weeks, I started to notice that they could sustain their attention in class longer than they previously could.

After a few weeks of consistently starting my class with a mindfulness practice, I forgot to do so one day. I was about to launch into the lesson when a few of my students raised their hands and said, "Wait, Mr. Habib, what about our mindfulness practice?" That was the moment I knew I was not going back. Our mindfulness time was an integral part of my lessons.

This led to an unintended benefit. Fewer students were tardy to my class because it can feel awkward to show up late to a room full of people who are totally silent.

The next by-product I didn't expect was that I started getting nice emails from parents! One mother emailed me and said, "Mr. Habib, I don't know what you are doing in your class but keep doing it. My son came home today and told me that I needed to self-regulate." I saved that one.

I also ended up *gaining* instructional minutes. Even though I technically had fewer minutes to teach the kids, the kids were much more focused, they could follow instructions more easily, and they weren't thinking nearly as much about what happened over lunch or about the test they were going to have in their next class. This became particularly important when we covered concepts that required a high cognitive load. Since they could sustain their attention for longer, they started asking better and better questions, and many of them were gentler with themselves when they didn't understand certain concepts, and they felt more ease with the process of learning.

Sumi's Growth through Mindfulness

Sumi was a sixteen-year-old girl in my Positive Psychology class. One day, about two months into the course, she arrived at class looking as if she had just uncovered the secret to living an amazing life. I was intrigued by her energy, and when it was her turn to share what she was grateful for in our gratitude circle, she said that she was grateful for the mindfulness exercises we had every day in class. In my mind I said, "Did she just say that?" I was incredibly excited to hear that, and my ego got a nice massage. Then, of course, my inner critic came in and said, "She's just trying to get a good grade. Relax, she doesn't really mean it." Luckily for me, my inner critic got put in its place as soon as Sumi explained why she was grateful for our mindfulness practices.

She said that she'd arrived at school feeling fine that morning. However, as soon as she got dropped off, she started to feel pressure right around her chest and stomach. Her first-period class was Biology, and as she was getting closer and closer to the class, she felt worse and worse. She decided to stop for a moment, take a deep breath, consciously notice what emotions were tied to these sensations, and then notice what thoughts were tied to these emotions. She realized that she felt a deep sense of fear and helplessness about the quiz she was about to take in that class. Even though she'd studied for many hours the night before, her inner critic started working on overdrive in her head. It asked her, "Why do you pretend to be any good at bio? Why did you even study for this quiz? Everyone else in this class is smarter than you. You're not only stupid in bio, but you're stupid for actually going to class on a quiz day. You should just cut class. Turn around. Why are you still walking toward a surefire F on a quiz?" The closer she got to her class, the louder the inner critic was yelling in her head.

She then shared something with the class that I will remember until the day I die. She said, "Mr. Habib, I took another deep breath in and walked toward a spot in the corner of the quad where I could be all alone. When no one else was around me, I closed my eyes, physically turned 180 degrees, and whispered to my inner critic, 'Hey, bud, I know you're trying to look out for me. I studied for this test, and you yelling at me is making me feel horrible. So I'm going to give you a hug now, and you're going to sit in the corner quietly because I have a quiz to take.'" She then imagined her inner critic getting some much-needed attention with a hug, sitting down quietly, and not bothering her anymore. She felt a moment of pride over her awareness and her ability to downregulate quickly. That was uplifting, and after taking another slow, soothing breath, she opened her eyes, turned around, and went to her Biology class feeling more peaceful and focused. She shared that this was the smoothest Biology quiz she'd ever had.

She told the circle that without our mindfulness practices, it would have been nearly impossible for her to be aware that it was her inner critic that was feeding her thoughts that caused her to experience helplessness, fear, chest pressure, and some nausea.

I was floored. What just happened? A sixteen-year-old girl just figured out that she could choose what thoughts to focus on and what beliefs to hold. What? It was a mic drop moment. I was speechless. I usually respond eloquently to what a student shares. After this share, all I could manage to say was, "Did you all hear and understand what Sumi just shared? Yes? Great. My job is done."

Mindfulness Practices to Deepen Your Students' Focus and Awareness

Many educators like the idea of practicing mindfulness exercises with their students but don't know where to begin. This leads them to feel unprepared and unsure of themselves. That's why I created a proven, step-by-step, quick-start approach to any mindfulness practice with students. You can use this template as a stand-alone practice or as a complement to the other mindfulness practice scripts in this chapter.

One of the most common mistakes educators make is that they want the mindfulness practice to be flawless for all their students. Don't strive for perfection. Your students might not feel completely peaceful. They might not even be completely quiet the entire time. That doesn't mean they're not practicing or that you're doing a bad job as a facilitator. The steps below will help you get into the practice easily.

1. In the morning, before your students show up to class, take thirty seconds to remind yourself why you believe this practice is important for your students' lives.

2. Take thirty seconds to visualize the practice going really well.

3. When your students are in their seats and you're ready to start the practice, say: "Good (morning/afternoon), everyone. We're going to start our class with a practice. If for any reason you need to sit this one out, you can read, write, or doodle quietly while the rest of us practice. Let's begin by finding our mindful body posture. Make sure your back is straight and your shoulders are relaxed. Uncross your arms and your legs. Put your hands on your knees with the palms of your hands facing up."

4. When your students are in their mindful body posture, say: "Our goal is to feel relaxed yet alert, so if you are not too tired, I invite you to close your eyes. If you don't want to close your eyes, keep them half open, gazing at the floor." (Note that younger children can be afraid of closing their eyes, so this step must be optional. And teenagers who haven't gotten enough sleep could easily drift off if their eyes are closed. They are more likely to stay alert if their eyes are slightly open.)

5. Slowly and more quietly, say: "Begin paying attention to your breath going in and out of your nostrils. Don't think about the breath; simply notice the sensation and temperature of the breath."

6. After they practice for thirty seconds, say: "And if you notice that you are not aware of your breath anymore, gently allow whatever thought, feeling, or sensation you are experiencing to float by, and bring your awareness gently back to your breath."

7. Sixty seconds later, offer them a second reminder to notice where their attention is.

8. At the conclusion of the practice, say: "Now take three deep breaths at your own pace. Relax your attention and slowly open your eyes."

9. Once your students have their eyes open, say: "Take a moment to notice how you are feeling right now. Is your brain calm? Is it active? Do you feel more relaxed? More tired perhaps? More focused? Whatever you feel is perfectly fine."

Mindfulness practices must be optional. Make it explicit that you are inviting them to participate in the practice and give them an "out" that is in alignment with your classroom expectations. This will send a message to your students that you care about them and respect them and that this is *their* practice. It is not another school assignment that they must do to get a good grade.

Sometimes educators ask me, "What if most of my students decide to opt out?" First, you should know that is rare. If you start with a few participants but stay consistent with the practices, you will likely see more students join in. That said, if you do notice that most (or all) of your students decide to sit it out, understand that's OK and that maybe it's just not a fit for most of the kids in that class. You can try it with your next class. This gives you a wonderful opportunity to accept this reality and any emotions that come up for you with gentleness, knowing that you are doing your best. Mindfulness practices can be strongly encouraged, but they should never be forced on anyone.

Keep in mind this is a secular practice, not a religious one. It is important to explicitly state to your students and their parents (during back-to-school night, for example) that the mindfulness practices you are inviting students to try are no different from working out at the gym. Instead of working out the muscles of the body, we're working out our brain so that we become more focused, relaxed, and resilient.

Our neural pathways are like our muscles. We train them, let them rest, and then train them slightly more intensely. This gradual approach is particularly important when we bring mindfulness practices into our classroom. Regardless of the age group you teach, I recommend starting with a three-second practice by teaching your students to take one mindful breath. The following day, do three breaths. Then, over the first two weeks, slowly work your way up to a minute of breathing. Then gradually work up to five-minute practices over the first two months. By the end of the first semester, you can do seven-minute to ten-minute practices with them.

Some somatic awareness and self-compassion practices can trigger past traumas, and it's important to teach all your students to first visualize a place where they feel safe, resourceful, and nurtured. This safe place needs to be established before delving into the practice, and students should always be given the option to stay in their safe place and not do the practice, or to come back to the safe place whenever they feel the need to do so. Here is an example of how to guide your students to create that refuge.

> Say: "In a moment I'm going to invite you into our practice, but first let's take time to create a safe and nourishing place for ourselves. Find a comfortable position on your chair with your back straight, the palms of your hands on your legs or your table, and your legs and arms uncrossed. Close your eyes and bring your awareness to your breath. Take five to ten deep breaths and begin to imagine a place that feels safe and nourishing to you. This can be an imaginary place or a real one. It can be indoors or in nature. Other people who you love and trust can be there, or you can be there by yourself. Imagine sitting in that safe, special place and being filled with caring, kind, gentle, and loving energy. Imagine this energy permeating your body. You can feel it in your veins, your muscles, your joints, your gut, your mind, and your heart, and it feels really good. Sit in that place with that energy for a minute, continuing to take deep breaths." (Give them a

minute, then continue.) "You are welcome to stay in this safe place for the rest of the exercise. If you do, continue to visualize healing, empowering, and safe energy coursing through your body. If you decide to participate in the practice, know that you can always come back to this place at any point. You get to decide."

What if you trigger something in them and then can't help them? This is a common fear for teachers, and there are a couple of important points that you must remember.

First, the suffering that student is experiencing is already there. With the practices and safe space that you offer, the student is no longer holding the suffering alone.

> With the practices and safe space that you offer, the student is no longer holding the suffering alone.

Second, if a student feels triggered, it is part of their healing journey, and without the practice, they could not even start the journey or discover the tools to support themselves.

Third, remember that you are not alone in caring for this child. And since you are not a mental health professional, it's your responsibility to seek help and collaborate with the school counselor, therapist, or administrator who can get them the additional help they may require.

Scripts for Impactful Mindfulness Practices

Each practice below has a script you can use to lead the practice followed by reflection questions you can ask your students to think-pair-share about afterward.

Closed-Focus Mindfulness Practices: Somatic Awareness

Mindful Breathing

> Today we're going to take a few mindful breaths. The difference between a regular breath and a mindful one is that when you breathe mindfully, you are fully aware of what is happening in your body as you breathe. For example, you might notice how your stomach rises with the inhalation and deflates with the exhalation. Or you might notice how your nostrils feel as you take the air in through your nose.
>
> We're going to bring our attention fully to our bodies. Don't think about the fact that you are taking a breath. Rather, feel the breath in your body.
>
> Find a comfortable position on your chair with your back straight, the palms of your hands on your legs or your table, and your legs and arms uncrossed. If you are not too tired, close your eyes. Otherwise keep your eyes half open and gaze at the floor. Now place one hand on your stomach. Then take (one, three, ten) mindful breaths at your own pace.

Notice when all students are done. Then tell them to repeat the same number of breaths one more time. Ask them to try to lengthen their out-breath slightly each time.

Reflection Questions:

- How did your mindful breath feel different from your regular breath?
- Which part of your body do you notice the most when you take a mindful breath?
- Did you notice any difference in how you felt when you lengthened your exhalations?

Noticing the Energy Inside Us

When we pay closer attention to our body, it is easier for us to have more control over our reactions and abilities, which gives us more control and peace in our lives.

Find a comfortable position on your chair with your back straight, the palms of your hands on your legs or your table, and your legs and arms uncrossed. I invite you to close your eyes and take three mindful breaths. *(Note that some young children may find closing their eyes scary, so it's important to make that optional.)*

With your eyes closed, and without moving your feet, pay attention to one of your feet, either the right or the left. Since it's not moving right now and your eyes are closed, how do you know that your foot is there? What sensations are you feeling right now in your foot?

Now bring your awareness to your hands and massage one of your hands with the other, keeping your eyes closed. You can massage the palm of your hand and your fingers. Do that for about thirty seconds at your own pace. What sensations do you notice? Does it feel cold or hot? Is it ticklish or soothing? What sensations do you experience now?

Now touch your table, shirt, and chair. (Give them some time in between each one.) What sensations do you notice as you touch these different textures?

Reflection Questions:

- What sensations did you notice?
- How could paying attention to the sensations in your body help you in your day-to-day life?

The Mindful Sloth

Use the QR code or go to eqschools.com/resources to access this resource.

Closed-Focus Mindfulness Practices: Cognitive Awareness

Noticing and Letting Go

Today we're going to practice noticing our thoughts without getting caught up in the stories behind them. Every time a thought comes to you, raise a finger as if you are going to say something, and then as soon as you drop the thought and come back to your breath, bring the finger back down. For example, if you are thinking about your next big test, instead of thinking about whether you should have studied more or comparing yourself unfavorably to your classmates, just notice that you thought about your test. Then raise your finger, and when you choose to let the thought go, drop your finger and come back to your breath. This will happen over and over again in your practice. See how many times you can be aware that a thought has come to you. Each time, allow it to float away before you get caught up in it, and come back to your breath.

Now find a comfortable position on your chair with your back straight, the palms of your hands on your legs or your table, and your legs and arms uncrossed. If you are not too tired, close your eyes. Otherwise keep your eyes half open and gaze at the floor. Take three deep, mindful breaths in and out. At your own pace, begin to bring your awareness fully to your breath.

When thoughts come to you, raise your finger and then allow the thoughts to float by. Drop your finger without getting caught up in the drama behind the thoughts, and bring your attention back to your breath. Bring your attention back to your breath gently, patiently, and nonjudgmentally.

Allow the students two to seven minutes to practice in silence. You may choose to remind them to bring their attention back to their breaths in the middle of the practice.

Reflection Questions:

- What thoughts did you notice come up repeatedly?
- When thoughts came up, how fast did you notice that you were no longer sensing your breath?
- Do you think that the skill of noticing your thoughts and choosing not to get sucked into them can be helpful for you? If so, why?

Sitting by the Waterway of Thoughts

Use the QR code or go to eqschools.com/resources to access this resource.

Noticing Our Judgmental Mind

Have you ever noticed you're judging yourself for one reason or another? For example, if you got a bad grade on a test, you might judge yourself to be lazy or stupid. There is nothing inherently good or bad about judging yourself or others. However, judging yourself harshly over time hurts your self-esteem and your well-being.

Today we're going to practice recognizing when our judgmental mind appears. Once you are aware that you are judging yourself, you have a choice. Do you continue to judge yourself or do you treat yourself with gentleness and kindness?

Some people think that treating themselves with gentleness after they did poorly on a test will only lead them to do poorly the next time. There is plenty of research that shows the opposite is true: when you treat yourself with kindness in the face of failure, you are significantly more likely to learn from the failure and to not repeat it again.

Today our only task is to notice when our mind begins to judge us for the way we conduct our mindfulness practice. To begin, find a comfortable position on your chair with your back straight, the palms of your hands on your legs or your table, and your legs and arms uncrossed. If you are not too tired, close your eyes. Otherwise keep your eyes half open and gaze at the floor. Take a few deep, mindful breaths, in and out, and allow yourself to feel relaxed yet alert.

Remain focused on your breath and let it be the anchor of your awareness for the next few minutes. When you recognize that you are no longer focusing on your breath, notice if your mind is judging you for practicing poorly. Is it saying that you are not doing a good job? That you are a scatterbrain? That everybody is doing it so much better than you? Or maybe it's just saying that this is too hard for you to do?

As soon as you recognize that your judging mind is active, visualize letting that voice float away and let yourself gently and nonjudgmentally come back to your breath.

You might need to do this hundreds of times, and that's OK. Just keep breathing in and out at your own pace. You're doing great.

Reflection Questions:

- How often did the judging mind pay you a visit during this practice? What did it say to you?
- How often does your judging mind pay you a visit during your day? What does it usually say to you?
- What is the benefit of recognizing when your judging mind is harsh with you?

From Gremlins to Self-Compassion

Before delving into this practice, remember to take students through the resourcing visualization first so that they have a safe place to come back to if necessary.

Sometimes our judging mind, known as a "gremlin," pays us a visit.

One of the most effective ways to deal with gremlins is to cultivate self-compassion. There is a lot of research showing that people who practice self-compassion after experiencing a setback or a disappointment build resilience faster than people who don't.

Before we begin the practice, I'd like you to think of a failure that you experienced recently or a time in the last few days when you beat yourself up. Please don't pick anything too traumatic or difficult, as it's better to practice with something smaller. (Give them a minute to think.)

In a moment I'm going to invite you to think about how your gremlin talked to you when you experienced the setback and how you felt, but first you're invited to find a comfortable position on your chair with your back straight, the palms of your hands on your legs or your table, and your legs and arms uncrossed. I invite you to close your eyes and bring your awareness to your breath. Take five to ten deep breaths and begin to imagine a place that feels safe and nourishing to you. (Take your students through the visualization resource on page 120 and give them a minute.)

I invite you now to recall what your gremlin was telling you when you experienced the failure. What was their tone of voice? What did it look like? Only recall this if you feel comfortable going there. (Give them thirty seconds to remember.)

Now remember this important message: Your gremlin is not you. It's a voice that you picked up somewhere, but it's not you. Your compassionate self is always stronger than your gremlin. So, let's get into our self-compassion practice.

Take a few deep, mindful breaths, in and out, and allow yourself to feel relaxed yet alert. Remain focused on your breath and let it be the anchor of your awareness for the next few moments.

Now again recall your setback, and as you do, place one hand on your heart and the other hand on top of that hand and continue to breathe normally. See if you can intentionally radiate compassion and warmth from your hands to your heart over the next few moments. If at any point this feels like too much, you can get back to your safe place and stay there. Only come back when you feel ready.

Now think of a kind word or sentence that you can repeat to yourself. For example: "This is hard to deal with, but I'm here for you and together we'll get through this. I'm not leaving." Repeat this mantra as you breathe in and out. If you feel up to it, add a term of endearment: "Sweetie, this is really tough and I'm here for you. I'm not leaving." If that feels too cheesy or unnatural, you can choose another word, such as *dude* or *bro*.

For the next few moments, repeat this kind mantra to yourself. (Give them a minute or two.)

Now take three deep breaths, and when you are ready, you may slowly open your eyes.

Reflection Questions:

- There is a famous saying by Rabbi Hillel: "If I'm not for myself, who will be for me? And if not now, then when?" What do you think he meant by this?

- What difference did you notice in your body when you put your hands on your heart and began to practice self-kindness?

Open-Focus Mindfulness Practices: Mindful Listening

For this practice, choose a piece of music that has no lyrics and that lasts between three and seven minutes. Some possible choices for music are Pachelbel's Canon in D or "Now We Are Free" from the *Gladiator* soundtrack, among many others.

> For our mindfulness practice today we're going to try something new. Instead of focusing on our breath or our body the whole time, we're going to mindfully listen to some music. Have you ever just sat down and listened to music without being in a car, or talking to your friends, or doing something else? How was that for you? (Take a few student responses.)
>
> In a minute I'm going to play a piece of music for you, and I ask that you fully bring your awareness to the music. Don't worry about any other sound, and if thoughts come to you, simply let them float by as soon as you're aware that you are no longer listening to the music. Then, gently and nonjudgmentally, come back to the music.
>
> To begin, find a comfortable position on your chair with your back straight, the palms of your hands on your legs or your table, and your legs and arms uncrossed. If you are not too tired, close your eyes. Otherwise keep your eyes half open and gaze at the floor. Take a few deep, mindful breaths, in and out, and allow yourself to feel relaxed yet alert.
>
> Keep breathing in and out, noticing your inhalation, the space between the inhalation and exhalation, and the entire length of the exhalation. I will play the music shortly, and when I do, allow yourself to be fully immersed in it. (After a minute has passed, start the music and let it play to the end.)

Keep breathing for another thirty seconds, taking deep inhalations and releasing slow exhalations. And when you are ready, you may slowly open your eyes.

Reflection Questions:

- What is the difference between listening to a piece of music mindfully and listening while doing something else?
- What emotions, sensations, visions, or thoughts came up for you as you were listening to the music?
- How can you use music in your life to help you, whether it's to regulate you, pump you up, or for other purposes?

Open-Focus Mindfulness Practices: Mindful Seeing

Use the QR code or go to eqschools.com/resources to access resource for the following practices:

- Opening Our Eyes (for Real)
- Loving Kindness
- Sending Love

Classroom Games and Activities That Foster Students' Awareness

COUNTING TO TEN. Students stand in a circle. As a group, students are to count sequentially from one to ten, but each student can say only one digit at a time, and if two people count at the same time, the group starts back at zero. Students should not count in the order that they are standing in the circle. Anyone, at any point, can count, as long as it's only one digit at a time. Allow at least seven tries, as most groups don't get it right away. After the fifth try, encourage the group to take a deep breath together, and before you get started, have participants silently look at one another and experience the energy that the group has formed. Then invite them to do the same but more slowly and to be sensitive and attuned to one another. Once the group is successful, you can have them do it with their eyes closed. If they want to take it to the next level, challenge them to do the ABCs. If the group is unsuccessful, you can celebrate that failure by all raising your arms and yelling "Woohoo!" together. Try again the next day.

PASS THE CLAP (WOOHOO!). Ask your students to stand in a circle with you. Tell them that you are going to clap, then the person to your right will clap, and then the person to their right will clap, etc., until everyone in the circle claps. Then tell the group that you are going to pass the clap in less than (however many) seconds. If you have thirty participants, shoot for less than ten seconds at first.

Say go and start a timer. The person to your right will clap, then the next person, etc. When the clap goes around the circle, stop the timer and let the group know how fast they did it. Note that this is a great opportunity to introduce the idea of celebrating failure. You can all raise your arms and yell "Woohoo!" together if you fail. This leads people to laugh and to feel more at ease. And if the group is successful, make the challenge a little harder. Maybe now the clap has to go around in seven seconds.

For an instructional clip of this game, use the QR code or go to eqschools.com/resources to access this resource.

MIRROR DANCING. Place participants in pairs and tell them to face each other but leave a space between them (about a foot). Have them imagine that they are each other's mirror. At your signal, students should do their best to exactly match the movement of their partner. Have one student (student A) start leading, and after a few minutes, prompt them to switch leadership to student B. Switch back and forth a few times, shortening the intervals, and eventually let them share leadership. Then play a slow, soothing song, and have them do the same exercise to that song for about sixty seconds. Finally, play a fun, upbeat song, and have them do the same exercise.

FIND ALL THE CIRCLES. Use the QR code or go to eqschools.com/resources to access this resource.

CAMERA GAME. Use the QR code or go to eqschools.com/resources to access this resource.

RELATIONSHIPS
FOR ACTIVITIES WITH STUDENTS GO TO PAGE 78

Use the pillars of attuned communication: drop in with presence, notice nonverbal cues, get curious, reflect back, empathize, and acknowledge. *(Page 25)*

Name your inference using the three-step method. *(Page 40)*

Respond to students' bids for attention. *(Page 47)*

Use active listening with students when they own the problem. *(Page 58)*

Send an I-message when you own the problem by using the three-step approach. *(Page 63)*

R

AWARENESS
FOR ACTIVITIES WITH STUDENTS GO TO PAGE 130

Use the practice for regulated breathing. *(Page 99)*

Use the practice for focused breath and noticing thoughts. *(Page 99)*

Use the 4 Ns Strategy: notice, name, normalize, nurture. *(Page 106)*

A

FOUR

ADVANCEMENT

BOLD GOALS, FIERCE GROWTH, PASSIONATE PATH

To realize one's destiny is a person's only real obligation and when you want something, all the universe conspires in helping you to achieve it.

—Paulo Coelho

Advancement is another way of saying personal growth. It occurs when we develop the courage and growth mindset to pursue our passions and to become the person we want to become. It happens when we understand that personal growth is not just a nice goal to have—it's a human necessity for thriving. It is what allows us to get out of bed energized each morning.

In this chapter, we're going to delve into how our personal development supports our teaching, and I'll take you through a simple step-by-step process to develop, pursue, and accomplish your personal growth goals. You'll also get practical activities to support your students' personal growth in the classroom.

Personal growth goals don't have to be about external accomplishments. Deciding to learn how to be more at peace and happier with the mundane in life is a solid personal development goal. So is deciding to become a better parent or a more effective teacher. You may have four little kids at home, and the biggest personal development goal you can take on now is to work out regularly so you can stay sane and healthy.

Any intrinsic and exciting desire that leads you to grow is valid and can be turned into an achievable goal. Starting a side business, coaching other teachers, becoming a principal or superintendent—these are all valid personal (not just professional) development goals if they come from pure internal desire. The key is to not let your gremlin or other people stop you from becoming the person you want to become.

The world needs people who are on fire about work and life. If being in the classroom is what does it for you, that's beautiful, and there are a million ways to grow as a teacher. If you feel called to pursue a leadership role at your school or district, that's also beautiful. Listen to your heart and your gut on this one. Not other people.

How Does Advancement Tie into Effective Teaching?

People who are passionate about work and life are much more effective educators. Why? Because this creative energy magnetizes students; they want to spend time with these educators. It feels good to be taught by someone who models being an excited lifelong learner. Even if your growth journey isn't related to teaching, becoming the person you want to become will positively impact your teaching (and other parts of your life) because you'll be happier and more energetic.

What if you feel uninspired? Are you a bad teacher? Not at all!! Every educator falls into a rut at one point or another in their career. Powerful educators notice they're in a rut and instead of beating themselves up, they celebrate the fact that they recognized it. Then they get curious about it, nonjudgmentally, and explore what may help them get out of it. Whether you're in a rut or not, the steps I outline below will help you grow into the person and professional you want to become—and have fun while doing so.

Practical Practices to Propel Your Growth

Step 1: Give Yourself the Permission to Dream

Martin Luther King Jr. (a hero of mine and I imagine yours as well) did not say "I have an idea" or "I have a plan." He said, "I have a dream."

To live the life of our dreams, we must first take time to dream.

We live in a society that values being practical and realistic, a society in which dreamers and idealists are considered detached, airy-fairy individuals. We are told from an early age to get a job that puts food on the table and to keep our feet on the ground. By the time we reach adulthood and settle into a practical and "realistic" job, the idea of dreaming can seem ridiculous and naïve. Here's what society isn't telling us (but that positive psychology research does tell us): Humans need to be both realistic and idealistic. And the two do not need to be in opposition. In fact, they complement each other and allow us to be true to our real nature.

Furthermore, anything that's ever been created by humans had to first be imagined. It's the practical dreamers that create and lead the world we all live in.

> It's the practical dreamers that create and lead the world we all live in.

If you were burned in the past, whether by your district's decision to not support a program you wanted to create or by an administrator not backing you up, it's hard to trust and to want to dream. I encourage you to first acknowledge that this is where you are and to use self-compassion as a tool to move through it. Then ask yourself, "What is a little dream that excites me and is within my control?"

Think of your dreaming process as your GPS. Without it, you are either stuck or traveling aimlessly through your life without a sense of direction. Of course, if you don't have any fuel in your car, the GPS won't do you any good. The fuel is the practical steps you need to take and the effort you need to put in to live the life that you really want.

We each need a vision that excites us, that pulls us toward it. Dreaming clarifies our desire, and that desire sharpens our focus. We can't get there unless we decide to carve out time and commit to the process of dreaming. So how do we do that?

WRITING EXERCISE #1: First, ask yourself how committed you are to this process. It's one thing to say that taking time to dream is important and it's another to actually do it. So on a scale of 1 to 10, how committed are you to setting aside a ten-minute session for this in the next week?

If the answer is less than 9, you will most likely not do it. That doesn't mean there is anything wrong with you; it just means that it's not a priority for you. If that's the case, I invite you to get curious about why. What is getting in the way of you taking that time? Perhaps it feels selfish? Understand that if you are happier and excited about your personal growth, people around you are more likely to feel that as well—that energy will rub off on them because emotions are contagious. If there are other issues keeping you from taking the time to dream, I encourage you to journal about them and get curious about each one without judging yourself.

WRITING EXERCISE #2: Once your commitment level is at 9 or 10, ask yourself where and when you are going to perform this exercise. Will it be in your room? Living room? Classroom? Office? At what exact time? Spaciousness is important because feeling relaxed is key when dreaming. Decide when you are going to do it, write it down, and commit to doing it.

Step 2: Focus on the Right Thing

It's important that you focus in the right direction. Most of us focus on what we want to achieve or attain. In his book *Atomic Habits*, James Clear shows that to experience long-lasting change, it's more powerful to focus on who we want to become than on certain goals or outcomes.[1] This is because we are a lot more intrinsically motivated to form positive new habits when we consider them a part of our identity. We are much more likely to learn a musical instrument if we consider ourselves a musician than if we just have a goal of picking up the guitar. The reason this is so important is because our beliefs about ourselves drive our behavior.[2]

Clear gives the example of two people who are trying to quit smoking. He writes: "When offered a smoke, the first person says, 'No thanks. I'm trying to quit.' It sounds like a reasonable response, but this person still believes they are a smoker who is trying to be something else. They are hoping their behavior will change while carrying around the same beliefs. The second person declines by saying, 'No thanks. I'm not a smoker.' It's a small difference, but this statement signals a shift in identity. Smoking was a part of their former life, not their current one. They no longer identify as someone who smokes."

That "small difference" is everything when it comes to setting the foundation for effective, long-lasting change in behavior because a behavior that is not in alignment with your identity will not stick. If being physically fit is a part of your identity, you will not need to convince yourself to get on the treadmill. If you consider yourself frugal, you will save. Conversely, if you tell yourself "I'm always late," you will be late. "I'm lazy" means you won't get much done. That is why we need to be careful with our inner (and outer) self-talk. What we tell ourselves becomes our belief about our identity, and that shapes our behavior.

Our beliefs about
ourselves drive
our behavior.

> A behavior that is not
> in alignment with your
> identity will not stick.

Instead of asking what outcomes you want to achieve, ask yourself what kind of person you want to become. This is your identity goal.

Ideas for identity goals:

- I want to become a person who experiences work-life balance regularly. (Tell yourself this instead of "I want to have less work.")
- I want to become a person who is physically fit. (Tell yourself this instead of "I want bigger muscles.")
- I want to become a leader (at my department, in my school, etc.).
- I want to become a person who embraces technology.
- I want to become a faster grader.
- I want to become a creative person.
- I want to become an entrepreneur.
- I want to become a person who has fun regularly.
- I want to become a more present and available parent (or partner).
- I want to become a person who travels the world regularly.
- I want to be an author.
- I want to become the type of person who attracts a life partner who is healthy for me.

WRITING EXERCISE #3: What kind of person do you want to become? Take five to ten minutes to journal about that. If more than one answer comes to you—for example, you want to become a more present parent, a traveler, and a leader—write all of these down.

Now rank them in order of importance. To increase the likelihood of effective change, stick to the top one on the list.

Ask yourself what kinds of things a person like that does. Freewrite or list bullet points for five minutes. What does a more present parent do to be more present with their children? What does a person who is fit do to make it easy for them to get to the gym?

Before starting EQ Schools, I allowed myself to play with the notion that I could become a speaker and entrepreneur, even if I only half believed it. Then I asked myself, "What does a public speaker do?" Here is a list of items I came up with:

- Speaks at as many conferences as they can (for free to get experience and build a brand and credibility)
- Networks with people who they can learn from and with
- Learns speaking strategies from mentors to engage the audience
- Manages their energy so they can perform at a high level while onstage

Next, I asked myself, "What does an entrepreneur do?"

- Takes calculated risks
- Learns how to sell their service in a way that feels good to their customer
- Finds strategic partners to collaborate with
- Develops their brand

After freewriting or making your own list, give yourself a precise amount of time to turn into that person. It could be months or years, but once you figure out the time frame, write down the date by which you will accomplish this identity goal.

This part can often throw people off because they don't want to "fail" at meeting their deadline. If that's you, understand that this process is meant to train your subconscious mind to believe you will become the person you want to become—and not in your next lifetime! As soon as you set your mind on a definite path, establish a firm timeline, and develop faith in your success, you'll begin to change your behavior faster than you can imagine, and it will be easier than you think.

That faith is developed by writing a personal growth oath and visualizing it, then reading it with emotion twice daily.

As a side note, I find that even if I do miss the deadline for my identity goal, I still make tremendous progress that I wouldn't have if I hadn't set myself a deadline.

If need be, you can extend the deadline and do your best to meet this new one.

Step 3: Write Your Personal Growth Oath

Your personal growth oath is an affirmation that creates certainty in your conscious and subconscious brain. It moves us from wishing that we could achieve our identity goal to knowing that we will. Its purpose is to show your conscious and subconscious mind that you have the resourcefulness to make it happen and it's only a matter of commitment, action, and time before it's done.

The oath has five parts to it.

1. The date of completion
2. The identity goal
3. A few actions you are going to take to achieve it
4. The positive impact this will have on others
5. An assertion of your faith in yourself—this goal will definitely be met when you do what you agreed to do

EXAMPLE #1: By October 2, 2023 (date), I will become a much more present and attuned parent for my children (identity goal). I will become that parent by meditating every day, by intentionally setting aside time at the beginning of every week to play with my kids, by setting a daily reminder for myself to get genuinely curious about my children's experience and to slow down when I listen to them, by establishing connection rituals during dinner time, and by reading this oath twice daily, when I wake up and before going to sleep (actions). This will allow my children to feel more seen, and it will help us feel happier and more connected (impact). My faith is strong, and because of that, I know I'm already a more present and attuned parent. I can see my kids' smiles, hear their laughter as we connect, and feel their bodies as I hug them. All of this is just waiting to happen when I do what I agreed to do (assertion).

EXAMPLE #2: By August 1, 2025, I will be a principal at a school. I will become that by getting my administrative credential, by networking with administrators at my district and other districts, by applying for leadership roles, by leading projects at my school every semester, and by reading this oath twice daily, when I wake up and before going to sleep. Students, parents, and my colleagues will benefit from my service and support, and I will be challenged and grow in new and exciting ways. My faith is strong, and because of that, I know I'm already a principal. I can see my colleagues listening to me in a staff meeting, I can hear kids and parents thanking me for supporting them, and I can experience how good it feels to be responsible for creating a joyful, safe, and emotionally intelligent culture at my school. All of this is just waiting to happen when I do what I agreed to do.

EXAMPLE #3: By September 28, 2024, I will feel more consistently at peace even when I face adversity. I will do so by practicing yoga daily, by meditating daily, by soothing myself as soon as I recognize that I'm stressed, and by reading this oath twice daily, when I wake up and before going to sleep. By doing so, I will be at my best and be able to give my best to my loved ones, my students, and my friends. My faith is strong, and because of that, I know I'm already much more calm and at peace. I can see myself meditating, I know how good it feels to self-regulate successfully in the face of difficult emotions, and I can hear my friends and loved ones telling me how much I've changed and how inspired they are by that. All of this is just waiting to happen when I do what I agreed to do.

> **WRITING EXERCISE #4:** Write your personal growth oath. Don't try to make it perfect, as it will morph over time anyway. Be sure to include all five components.

Step 4: Visualize

Martin Luther King Jr. said, "I have a dream," and then he proceeded to describe his dream in detail because he took the time to visualize that dream in detail in the first place. Visualizing the result of your growth oath, with emotions, cements it in your subconscious. It tricks your brain into believing that something that hasn't been accomplished yet has been accomplished.[3] To understand what happens biologically and neurologically when we visualize, use the QR code or go to eqschools.com/resources to access this resource.

What are the steps to a powerful visualization?

STEP 1: FIND A QUIET PLACE. Find a room in your house where you will not be interrupted for a period of ten minutes. Then find a comfortable place to sit (ideally not on your bed), close your eyes, and take a few deep breaths through your nose.

STEP 2: LISTEN TO INSPIRING MUSIC. (This step is optional but recommended.) Music is incredibly powerful. It floods us with positive hormones that change our neurochemistry, and it generates strong emotions in us that cultivate a deeper commitment to our passion and desires. If you have noise-canceling headphones or earbuds, put them on and listen to a playlist of inspirational music that gets you going. Then open your eyes and read your personal growth oath with passion and determination. For a list of inspirational playlists, use the QR code or go to eqschools.com/resources to access this resource.

STEP 3: BE THE STAR AND ADD DETAILS. What do your surroundings look like when you've become the person you want to become? Who are you interacting with? How do they interact with you? How confident and at peace do you feel? How much fun are you having? Visualize this from your personal perspective, not from the viewpoint of an observer.

STEP 4: USE ALL YOUR SENSES. Make the experience as vivid as you can by involving sound, smell, and feel. If you want to become more fit, feel the dumbbells in your hands, hear your trainer encourage you to do one more set. If you want to be a more present parent, feel the softness of your child's sweater as you snuggle them. Fully immerse yourself somatically in the experience.

STEP 5: BATHE IN THE POSITIVE EMOTIONS. The power of visualization really starts taking shape when you allow yourself to move from your mind into your heart and your gut. Give yourself enough time to *feel*, not just think. This will infuse you with energy, open you to new possibilities, and attract what you desire.

STEP 6: THANK YOURSELF, THE UNIVERSE, THE SOURCE, OR G-D. If you don't believe in a higher power, thank yourself for having the courage to reach your full potential. Expressing gratitude to a higher source (if you believe in one) for something that hasn't happened yet reminds you that it has your back, and by acknowledging that power, you form a deep connection with it, which can soothe you when things get tough and give you momentum when things flow.

Step 5: Read Your Personal Growth Oath Twice Daily

Steps 1 through 4 can be done just once, though I highly encourage you to visualize (step 4) on a weekly basis, as it will infuse you with energy. Step 5 needs to be done twice daily, when you wake up and before you go to sleep. The timing is important because when you wake up and right before you fall asleep, you come closest to your subconscious mind. The daily consistency gives you the momentum to continue doing what you agreed to do and keeps you focused.

This is a very important part of the process, so don't skip it.

When you read your oath, read it with conviction and passion. Let yourself feel it—don't just go through the motions of reading it. Immerse yourself in it for a minute or two.

Step 6: Dance with Your Gremlin and Choose the Right Beliefs

Now that you've laid out your oath, the next step will ensure that you don't freeze up when it's time to implement it.

When we begin to act, we almost always get a visit from our gremlin. You know that inner critic in your head that tells you you're never enough? Otherwise known as the itty bitty shitty committee? Well, that voice loves to feed you cognitive distortions. They will be mostly false, but they may contain a grain of truth that deludes you into thinking the entire distortion is true.

Here's a common example. A teacher who is also a mother needs to stay late at work one day to finish grading some assignments. Her gremlin pays her a visit and says, "You are such a horrible mother!" (Notice the cognitive distortions here: black-and-white thinking, labeling, and overgeneralization.) This thought is obviously false, but this woman may believe it because she feels guilty for not being with her children this afternoon (the grain of truth). Instead of buying into it, she could realize that she is usually with her kids at an earlier hour, and this makes her an amazing mother, and sometimes the life of a teacher requires her to put in longer hours at school. It can be an opportunity for her kids to entertain themselves and become more self-sufficient. The key is to first realize that the gremlin is there, and with that awareness we can choose how to respond to it.

Our gremlin is going to show up. It will never fully go away because, in a way, it's trying to protect us. It just does it ineffectively and in a way that ends up hurting us. It keeps you smaller than you ought to be, and the rest of the world doesn't get to benefit from your light fully shining. When we're aware that our gremlin is beating us up and feeding us false beliefs, instead of letting it derail us, we can dance with it, tame it, and gently let it go.

How do we do that? With a three-step approach: observing, soothing, and rewording.

WRITING EXERCISE #5: (This only needs to be done when your inner critic pays you a visit.) Take five to ten minutes to write (or even just think—though writing is better!) about the following:

Your gremlin loves to live in the back of your mind, and because it's in the background, you often don't even notice it's there. But when you slow down, get intimate with it, and write down what it says, you expose it. Then you can realize that not only is it wrong, but it often sounds ridiculous.

Take some time to notice and get intimate with your gremlin. Write about the following: What does your gremlin sound like? What exact words does it use? What tone does it use? Is it female? Male? Nonbinary? Is it one being or multiple beings? Does it remind you of someone from your past? Finally, give your inner critic a name. Don't skip that step. It will take a lot of its power away.

Take a moment to soothe yourself using the self-compassion practice in the "Awareness" chapter, on page 100. Once you feel more regulated, remember that the gremlin is not you. Try seeing it as a little child who is trying to get their needs met. Also remember that it's trying to protect you. Now write a gentle response to your gremlin using a mature, adult perspective. Something like: "I get that you are worried about (fill in the blank) and that you are trying to protect me. To be honest, you are causing more harm than good, so I'm going to give you a hug now to help you relax, and then you can go to the back seat. I'm going to drive the car from now on."

Imagine how your best friend (or someone who can speak tenderly while still being direct) would send you the message that your gremlin tried to send you. Write something like: "Sweetie, every teacher struggles from time to time, and the fact that you care about teaching more effectively is an amazing sign. There is plenty of time for you to reteach this, and I encourage you to seek help from a colleague who can give you some suggestions. Your students are lucky to have you!"

When you activate that level of kindness within yourself, your gremlin will be quiet, off in a corner of your mind, chillin' like a little villain without bothering you anymore.

Now that the gremlin is out of the way, you are ready to infuse yourself with the beliefs that will lead to your growth.

For a deeper look at the power of beliefs in shap-ing our life, our success, and our students' success, use the QR code or go to eqschools.com/resources to access this resource.

WRITING EXERCISE #6: As you think about the kind of person you want to become, take five to ten minutes to write down answers to the following questions:

- What beliefs do you have about yourself that empower you to become that person?
- What beliefs keep you from being that person?
- What new beliefs can you implant in your head that will empower you to become that person? (Hint: these are often the opposite of the disempowering beliefs you have.)

Let's look at some examples to make this more concrete.

Vision: I want to be able to balance my work and home life more effectively.

Current empowering beliefs that are helpful: I can be disci-plined about getting home on time when I put my mind to it.

I perform best and am happiest when I balance work and life effectively.

Current disempowering belief that is not helpful: If my colleagues stay at work longer than I do, it means I'm not as committed to my work as they are.

New empowering beliefs to adopt: I'm a committed teacher, and making sure I have time for myself and my loved ones makes me an even better teacher.

The number of hours I spend working after school does not indicate my level of commitment to my work.

Disempowering beliefs stop people from taking action. Do not skip this step.

Remember: You choose what to believe and hold on to as well as what to disbelieve and discard. Decide to be your own best coach.

Step 7: Commit

It's important that you be clear with yourself about how committed you are to becoming the person you want to become.

WRITING EXERCISE #7: Answer the following question honestly. On a scale of 1 to 10, how committed are you to becoming the person you want to become? If the answer is 9 or 10, move on to the next step. If it's lower than that, get curious about it. Do you need to tweak your identity goal? Do you need to pick a different identity goal that is more exciting? Are you afraid of something? Write without judgment. The more curious you can be, the better. You will find new truths that will allow you to get your personal growth oath just right.

WRITING EXERCISE #8: Once you are excited enough and your commitment level is at 9 or 10, add your empowering beliefs and level of commitment to the bottom of your personal oath.

You can do so with a simple phrase: "My faith is strong because I am (empowering belief number one), (empowering belief number two), and because I'm fully committed. I know that I am already (identity goal)."

Step 8: Create Rituals

To become the person you want to become and live with more passion, you will need to change your behavior. Much more than willpower, creating rituals that cultivate our growth is what leads to sustained behavioral change. Think about it this way: How many of your New Year's resolutions have you ever kept? Probably zero because it takes tremendous willpower. But how many days in the last year have you brushed your teeth? Hopefully the answer is 365. The sum of our rituals makes up how we live our lives and who we become.

> The sum of our rituals makes up how we live our lives and who we become.

WRITING EXERCISE #9: Write three or more rituals that will lead you to achieve your identity goal. Examples are:

- Wake up at 5:30 a.m.
- Work out daily in the morning
- Meditate
- Spend one hour a day educating myself
- Set an alarm clock for when to leave school
- Cut vegetables on Sunday for my meals for the week
- Play with my kids daily

It's one thing to know what rituals you want to have. It's another thing to actually do them regularly. How do we establish healthy rituals and discard unhealthy rituals?

To establish healthy rituals do two things:

1. Lower the activation energy that it takes you to engage in the ritual.
2. Make it visible.

To discard unhealthy rituals, do the opposite:

1. Increase the activation energy that it takes you to engage in the ritual.
2. Hide it.

	Activation Energy	Visibility
To establish healthy rituals	Lower	Make it visible
To discard unhealthy rituals	Increase	Hide it

Activation energy is the amount of energy it takes you to start the ritual.[4] If you want to start working out regularly in the morning, you can lower the activation energy to do that by sleeping in your gym clothes and having your sneakers right by your bed. If you want to learn to play violin, place the violin in your living room where you can easily grab it and play. This also makes the violin visible to you every time you pass it, sending you a quick reminder to pick it up when you are free to practice.

On the flip side, I have zero willpower when it comes to eating ice cream. If it's in my freezer, no matter how many times I tell myself not to eat it during the day, when 8:30 p.m. comes around, I'm tired and I have no willpower left. Guess what happens next? You got it. But with my new house rule of no ice cream in the freezer, if I really want ice cream at 8:30 p.m., I have to put my shoes on, get in my car, drive through a bunch of traffic to the ice cream shop, sit in my shame until I get there, and then pay for and eat the ice cream there. All of that requires a lot of energy, and I usually just give up on the ice cream idea. By increasing the activation energy, I have removed this unhealthy ritual from my life.

WRITING EXERCISE #10: In what way(s) can you lower the activation energy for the three rituals that you want to establish? How can you make them visible? Is there an unhealthy ritual that is keeping you from becoming the person you want to become? If so, how can you increase the activation energy for that ritual?

Step 9: Have a Bias toward Action

You learn so much more from doing than from thinking about doing. Your personal growth oath and the rituals you've established for yourself give you a plan of action that you should start right away. Don't wait. You will not do things perfectly the first time, but you will gather information on how to improve, and more importantly you will gather momentum.

Step 10: Celebrate the Little Victories

Achieving your identity goal is a process that usually takes some time. It requires many small steps to get there, and if you don't take the time to appreciate the little achievements, you can lose your motivation to continue. When you take a moment to emphatically celebrate small wins by yelling "Woohoo!" or patting yourself on the back, you engender a feeling of pride and joy that is paramount in keeping the momentum going and energizing yourself for the next step in the process. If I only got excited about writing this book when the book was finished, I would have never finished. It was too large a project, so I decided that every time I completed an hour-long writing session, I would celebrate with a yell, a pat on the back, or a dance! Get silly and have fun with it!

Journal Prompts That Cultivate Personal Development

- If I had the courage to be bold and do what I really wanted to do, what would I do more of? Who would I become?
- What is the risk of *not* making bolder moves toward what I really want in my life?
- What am I passionate about? How can I have more of that?
- Who has inspired me in the past? Why?
- What am I afraid of? How can I work on these fears?
- What is the main message that my gremlin feeds me? How long has this message kept me smaller than I am? How good would it feel to drop it and believe the opposite?
- Am I afraid to dream? If so, why?
- How have I successfully dealt with disappointment in the past?
- What do I prefer not having in my life? (Create a list and once you identify the top three things, write about how you can remove them from your life or experience a lot less of them.)
- Am I becoming the person I want to become?
- What is my legacy so far? What do I want it to be?

Igniting Students' Growth with Fun & Interactive Classroom Exercises

1-2-3. Pair people up. Have them face each other and decide who is partner A and who is partner B. Be sure to demonstrate the game with a volunteer first.

Partner A says "one." Partner B says "two." Partner A says "three." Then partner B says "one," partner A says "two," and partner B says "three." And so on. They keep going faster and faster until one person makes a mistake. When that happens, both people take responsibility for that mistake, and they both yell "Woohoo!" and raise their arms together.

After the group plays this game for forty-five seconds, get their attention and show the next version of this game. Instead of saying "one," the partners will clap. They will still say "two" and "three." Demonstrate this with a volunteer, then have the group play for forty-five seconds.

Then show them the next version. The partner will still clap on one, they will now snap instead of saying "two," and they will still say "three."

Let the group play for forty-five seconds, and then show them the last version of the game. Participants will clap on one, snap on two, and stomp on three. Demonstrate this with a volunteer, then have the group play for forty-five seconds. At the end of that round, tell the pairs to go back to saying one, two, and three. Let them do this for about ten seconds and see what happens. It will be much easier for them. It's important to remember to encourage the participants to celebrate their failures together with a "Woohoo!"

For an instructional clip of this game, use the QR code or go to eqschools.com/resources to access this resource.

PASS MULTIPLE CLAPS. Tell your students that you're going to play the same game as Pass the Clap (woohoo!) on age 131... except this time they'll pass multiple claps instead of just one. After the first clap passes one-quarter of the circle, you will clap again. When the second clap passes one-quarter of the circle, clap a third time. Three claps will be going around the circle. See whether all three claps get through the circle. It's common for a few students to pass the first clap but to not be aware another is coming, so before you pass the claps, remind them that multiple claps are coming. If a clap is lost midway through, everyone can celebrate that failure at the end with a "Woohoo!" Encourage your students to be fully present as you try the game again. If the group was successful in passing all three claps around, celebrate! For an extra challenge, pass five, six, or even seven claps around.

To see an instructional video clip of this game, use the QR code or go to eqschools.com/resources to access this resource.

FAILURE BOW. Use the QR code or go to eqschools.com/resources to access this resource.

Activities That Cultivate Personal and Intellectual Growth in Students

Growth-Mindset Activities and Exercises

Carol Dweck, who wrote the book *Mindset*, defines mindset as a self-perception or self-theory that people hold.[5] "I'm a good teacher" is a mindset. So is "I'm intelligent" or "I'm lazy." Our beliefs about ourselves have great consequences for our well-being and performance. The more aware we are of our self-perceptions, the more we can choose to move from a fixed mindset to a growth mindset. In a fixed mindset, people believe their basic qualities, like their intelligence or talent, are fixed traits that cannot be changed. In a growth mindset, people believe that their abilities can be developed through dedication and hard work and that their talents can be improved. The skill of moving from a fixed to a growth mindset is critical to learning.

Below are simple yet powerful growth-mindset activities for students.

Elementary School

THE POWER OF ADDING THE WORD YET. Add the word *yet* when your students say they can't do something. For example, if your student says, "I can't multiply three times nine," simply have them repeat what they said with the word *yet* at the end.

USE BOOKS. The following books are great for exploring the qualities of growth mindset: *Giraffes Can't Dance*; *Ish*; *The Girl Who Never Made Mistakes*; *Making a Splash*; *Beautiful Oops!*; *Everyone Can Learn to Ride a Bicycle*; and *The OK Book*. With each book, use a graphic organizer to write down growth-mindset takeaways.

POSITIVE SELF-IMAGE. Have students draw or write positive assertions about themselves and have them tape the results to their desks. That visual reminder will cultivate a growth mindset through the learning journey.

High School

GROWTH VERSUS FIXED MINDSETS CHALK TALK. Before teaching about growth versus fixed mindsets, post large easel papers around your room with a statement at the center of each. Give students markers and tell them to write whether they agree or disagree with the central statement and to explain why. Students can also respond to previous students' responses by drawing a circle and an arrow to their response. This is to be done completely silently. Example statements include:

- Being a good artist is a gift some people have and others do not.
- A person's intelligence cannot change.
- A person can improve in anything if they put their mind to it and make an effort.
- Talent is more important than effort when it comes to academic subjects.
- Getting feedback on my performance (in school, sports, etc.) is helpful.

After the students have written their responses, go around the room and jot down the ones you will use as prompts for a verbal discussion. Lead a discussion about these responses and write the major themes students have brought up on the board. Use these themes as a starting point when you teach them about growth versus fixed mindsets.

DEVOTE A LESSON TO GROWTH VERSUS FIXED MINDSETS. No matter what subject you teach, help students learn that they can choose to adopt a growth mindset at any time. Devote a lesson to this, and define the difference between the two mindsets. Show a graphic organizer of how fixed versus growth mindsets are expressed when it comes to challenges, effort, criticism, and others' success. Then have students journal about the following prompts:

- In which area of life are you more inclined to experience a growth versus fixed mindset?
- What specific beliefs lead you to have a fixed mindset? What emotions accompany those beliefs?
- What specific beliefs lead you to have a growth mindset? What emotions accompany those beliefs?
- What would be the benefits of adopting a growth mindset instead of a fixed one?
- What, if anything, stops you from adopting a growth mindset?

ATTITUDE JOURNAL. Use the QR code or go to eqschools.com/resources to access this resource.

RELATIONSHIPS
FOR ACTIVITIES WITH STUDENTS GO TO PAGE 78

Use the pillars of attuned communication: drop in with presence, notice nonverbal cues, get curious, reflect back, empathize, and acknowledge. *(Page 25)*

Name your inference using the three-step method. *(Page 40)*

Respond to students' bids for attention. *(Page 47)*

Use active listening with students when they own the problem. *(Page 58)*

Send an I-message when you own the problem by using the three-step approach. *(Page 63)*

AWARENESS
FOR ACTIVITIES WITH STUDENTS GO TO PAGE 130

Use the practice for regulated breathing. *(Page 99)*

Use the practice for focused breath and noticing thoughts. *(Page 99)*

Use the 4 Ns Strategy: notice, name, normalize, nurture. *(Page 106)*

ADVANCEMENT
FOR ACTIVITIES WITH STUDENTS GO TO PAGE 154

Take time to dream. *(Page 136)*

Focus on who you want to become. *(Page 138)*

Write your personal growth oath and repeat it daily. *(Page 142)*

Visualize the result of your growth oath. *(Page 144)*

Choose empowering beliefs. *(Page 146)*

Lower activation energy for healthy rituals. *(Page 152)*

FIVE

MEANING

DISCOVERING YOUR INNER DRIVE

The more one forgets himself—by giving himself to a cause to serve or another person to love—the more human he is.

—Victor Frankl

Stop Searching for Meaning—Recreate It

Experiencing meaning in life is a prerequisite for genuine, long-term happiness. But it's important to understand that you don't *find* meaning—you actively *create* meaning.[1] You can create meaning through your love for someone else, through accomplishing things, and through transforming any suffering that you experience into growth.

We need to recreate meaning over and over again in our life, since what is most meaningful to us changes as we age. For example, I experienced a lot of meaning when I created and taught my Positive Psychology class for high schoolers, and I experienced it again when I founded my company, EQ Schools, and provided workshops for educators. And while I still experience meaning from leading workshops, retreats, and conferences, I also create much of my meaning by spending time with my children, planning experiences for us, going to their

You don't *find* meaning—
you actively *create* meaning.

dance and flag football classes, laughing together at the dinner table, and being there for them when they experience difficult emotions.

Since so much of our time and energy is spent at work, we get a special boost in well-being when we create meaning at our jobs. Why do you do what you do? And does your *why* provide you with the belief that your life has value and significance? How does being connected to your meaning tie into effective teaching?

While educating and leading others is inherently meaningful, I've met countless educators who have lost the fire for teaching. It is critical for us as educators and leaders to intentionally recreate meaning throughout our careers instead of operating on autopilot and hoping to "find meaning."

In my fifth year of teaching, I began to feel bored. While I enjoyed connecting with a new crop of students every year, I felt agitated because I was teaching the same subject, my routine felt stale, and my creative juices had dried up. I needed a gentle kick in the pants, so that summer, I enrolled in a two-week PD program that reinvigorated me and helped me recreate my meaning as a teacher. Being newly inspired, I decided to share with my students that I teach because I want to make the world a better place. I shared my experience of being discriminated against. I told them how important it was for me to teach them about history and how to avoid repeating atrocities from the past, how to celebrate people who are different as opposed to judging them. My students could feel the energy behind my words, and this engaged them.

Students can tell when we lack meaning in what we do. Conversely, they appreciate the creative energy that comes when we recreate meaning in our work.

If you find that you are lacking meaning at work (or in life), do the following:

- Acknowledge it. By explicitly owning it, you lessen the energy drain caused by frustration, and you can be ready to actively recreate meaning.

- Give yourself permission to find meaning in things other than teaching, like the arts, politics, or your kids. It's 100 percent OK if teaching is not the endeavor that brings you the most meaning at this moment. Remember that students benefit most from teachers who are passionate about life and excited to wake up every day. So the more you give yourself permission to be excited about other things, the better you'll feel, and the more students will benefit. If this means that you will eventually switch careers, that's 100 percent OK as well. That will pave the way for you to be passionate about your new work, and you'll make room for another person who is stoked about teaching. Do not feel any guilt about that. The world needs more people who are on fire about what they do.

The world needs more people who are on fire about what they do.

- Be gentle with yourself. I don't know any educator who goes through their entire career completely connected to their meaning and purpose. It's OK to feel stuck, bored, or frustrated.
- Be patient with yourself. Recreating meaning is a process that can take some digging and some time. While you should actively recreate meaning, you shouldn't push for it.
- Look for professional or personal development programs that sound inspiring to you. They may be the kindling you need to recreate meaning.

Try the following exercises to expedite the process.

WRITING EXERCISE #1: Ask yourself, "What does life expect of me now?"[2] Freewrite for five to ten minutes without stopping. Then look back at your journal and write for another five minutes about the following: Out of what you wrote, what is most exciting for you? What emotions are coming up for you? Who do you need to become to do what life expects of you?

Optional (but highly recommended): Go through the ten steps for fun personal growth from the "Advancement" chapter to create your personal growth oath to achieve your identity goal.

WRITING EXERCISE #2: It's helpful to be connected to the unique story of why you became an educator or administrator. When I ask educators why they do what they do, they often respond, "We do it for the kids." That's lovely, but it's also a bit too broad a response to recreate meaning. Freewrite about the following: What is the primary reason you became an educator? Did you always know you wanted to be a teacher? If so, why? What about teaching was so compelling to you? If not, did anything happen when you were a student that led you to decide to teach? What is your story? The more detail the better—it's kindling for the fire of why you do what you do, and it will help you recreate meaning. For an example of my own journal entry, use the QR code or go to eqschools.com/resources to access this resource.

WRITING EXERCISE #3: Recreating meaning comes from being in touch with how good it feels to use our talents and gifts to give to others. Freewrite about the following: In what ways do you love to give to others, whether it's your students, colleagues, or students' parents? What are you talented in? This is no time to be modest. You are writing just for yourself, so go crazy—gush about yourself as much as you want. It's actually an important skill to develop so you can see yourself for all that you are. Don't worry, you're not going to turn into a self-centered schmuck. Have fun!

Journal Prompts to Create and Deepen Meaning

- What are the most meaningful parts of my day-to-day work? How can I have more of these moments?
- Besides teaching, why am I here? What does life expect from me?
- I feel most alive when . . .
- The last time I was so immersed in what I was doing that I lost track of time was . . .
- How do I want to be remembered?
- Who do I matter to? In what ways do I matter to them? Who matters to me the most? Why?

Cultivating Meaning for Students

In *The Palgrave Handbook of Positive Education*, M. F. Steger et al. share that when helping our students to experience more meaning in their lives, it's important to move away from the abstract question

"What is the meaning of life?" Instead, we should focus on the ability to cultivate a sense of life's meaning.[3]

Two research studies showed that there are three dimensions of meaning in life:[4]

1.   Coherence: Who am I? How do I experience the world around me? And how do I fit into the world?
2.   Purpose: What am I most motivated by? What are my core, intrinsic goals?
3.   Significance: Do I matter to others? Am I worthy? Do I bring value to others?

Practical Exercises/Activities That Deepen a Sense of Coherence

VIA Character Strengths Survey with Reflection Questions

The Values in Action Character Strengths Survey was developed by Martin Seligman, who is considered the father of positive psychology. The purpose of the survey is to show participants what their strengths are and how they can manifest them in the world.

Provide these instructions to your students and have them journal about the reflection questions at the bottom.

1.   Go to the VIA Institute on Character website and read about the twenty-four character strengths included on the VIA survey.[5] (Provide students with a current link.)
2.   Go to the "Authentic Happiness" page on the University of Pennsylvania's website.[6] (Provide students with a current link.)
3.   Scroll down to the VIA Strength Survey for Children and click the Take Test button on the right side.
4.   This will take you to a log-in page. Underneath the Username and Password boxes, select Register.

5. Create an account.

6. Go back to the VIA Strength Survey for Children.

7. Take the survey.

8. At the end of the survey, you will see what your top character strengths are. Write the top five in your journal, making sure to copy the entire description for each.

9. Write a journal entry using these prompts: Does it make sense to you that these are your top five character strengths? Was anything surprising to you? How could you use your top three character strengths to experience more fulfillment? Think of a tangible way in which you can use your top character strength this week and describe it in your journal. What else did you learn from doing this assessment?

Practical Exercises/Activities That Deepen a Sense of Purpose

Exploring Self-Concordant Goals

Self-concordant goals are aligned with who we are and what we really want to do with our lives.[7] They are not necessarily easy to reach, but pursuing them generally feels fulfilling.

Provide the definition of self-concordant goals to your students and then have them journal about the following prompts:

- What are your core, intrinsic goals?
- Pick your most important goal that is not easily reachable. What steps must you take to get there?
- How do you stay motivated in the face of obstacles, fatigue, or apathy?

*Developing an Optimistic
Explanatory Style*

Use the QR code or go to eqschools.com/resources
to access this resource.

Practical Exercises/Activities That Deepen a Sense of Significance

Prosocial Behavior Prompts—Think-Pair-Share

Have students journal about the following prompts:

- How can I be of service to others at my school? What are small things I can do?
- In what ways can I help others feel that they belong?
- How can I help reduce or stop bullying in my school (including cyberbullying)?

Then have students pair up and share their responses. After three to five minutes, lead a class discussion about these prompts and write main ideas on the board.

Follow up by asking students which of these ideas they are willing to act on. On a scale of 1 to 10, how committed are they to acting? Finally, ask them to pick a date and time to follow through.

Who Is in My Universe of Obligation?

Use the QR code or go to eqschools.com/resources
to access this resource.

Impactful Activities That Combine Coherence, Purpose, and Significance

Powerful Introduction

The powerful introduction activity is a classic positive psychology exercise that has been used in many settings with significant results.[8] Students will introduce themselves to their peers by reading a true autobiographical story. This exercise is most effective in the beginning of the year or semester but can also be done throughout the semester by spreading out student shares over time. Note that this exercise does take time but is definitely worth doing no matter what subject or grade level you teach (as you'll see from one of my student testimonials below). I provide answers to common concerns or questions about this exercise at eqschools.com/resources. Or you can use the QR code on this page to access this resource.

Provide the following instructions to your students:

Introduce yourself to the class by writing a story about your past, present, and future. Writing this story can help you find meaning and value in your experiences. People who develop empowering stories about their lives tend to experience a greater sense of meaning, which can contribute to personal growth and well-being. The length of your introductory story needs to be at least three minutes and at most five minutes.

NOTE: We are not interested in achievement or performance but rather strength of character, what your struggles might be or have been, and how you've overcome them or are currently coping with them.

Write the story of your past. Be sure to describe challenges you've overcome and personal strengths that allowed you to prevail.

Describe your life and who you are now. How do you differ from your past self? What are your strengths now? What challenges are you facing? (As a reminder, every person on earth faces challenges and the difficult emotions that come with them. I encourage you to write about these without censoring yourself. You do not need to share everything you wrote with the rest of the class. You can share just what you feel comfortable sharing.)

Write about your ideal future. How will your life be different from what it is now? How will you be different from your present self?

Give your students a week to complete this exercise. Then you can devote two class periods to sharing these stories one at a time, or you can spread out the stories over the first month of class. Anytime someone shares a story, you should ideally have your students sit in a circle.

Set some guidelines before students start sharing. Examples are:

- Listen attentively, quietly, and supportively.
- Keep whatever is said here confidential.
- Allow yourself to feel as vulnerable as you're willing to be.

This exercise is profound. You will see students opening to one another, willing to show vulnerability, and it will create a deeper sense of emotional resonance and meaning for all of them. As my student Sean (not his real name) wrote in his journal:

"Every day I sit down in class, and I look around and I see people are so very . . . human. I see people acting more friendly and tender than I ever expected. I see them put their pride outside and show us really what's up. I see people trusting one another. For the first time,

I've shared with a group about my fear of being a less-than-good person and I felt so safe."

Sean experienced more meaning and felt happier and more at peace. He'd struggled academically beforehand because he didn't feel that he belonged at school and was constantly disengaged. After this exercise, he was on fire academically. He asked amazing questions, brought up great points during discussions, turned in his assignments on time, and nailed the assessments. This changed the trajectory of his experience at school and in life.

A final point: Before starting this powerful introduction exercise, it's crucial for you to remind students that you are a mandated reporter. You must let them know that if they share something involving grave physical or psychological danger (if they're being hurt by someone else, hurting themselves, or hurting someone else), legally, you must report this to other professionals. This will deepen the trust that students feel, because they now understand the rules of the game and they get to decide what they are willing to share.

My Life Sketch

Use the QR code or go to eqschools.com/resources to access this resource.

If you do experience plenty of meaning in your life and work, that's awesome. Now you're on your way to helping your students create authentic meaning for themselves. This is crucial because children's anxiety and psychological distress is at an all-time high and increasing at an alarming rate. Teaching students to create meaning in their day-to-day experience leads them to be happier and more resilient and to perform better academically.

RELATIONSHIPS

FOR ACTIVITIES WITH STUDENTS GO TO PAGE 78

Use the pillars of attuned communication: drop in with presence, notice nonverbal cues, get curious, reflect back, empathize, and acknowledge. *(Page 25)*

Name your inference using the three-step method. *(Page 40)*

Respond to students' bids for attention. *(Page 47)*

Use active listening with students when they own the problem. *(Page 58)*

Send an I-message when you own the problem by using the three-step approach. *(Page 63)*

R

AWARENESS

FOR ACTIVITIES WITH STUDENTS GO TO PAGE 130

Use the practice for regulated breathing. *(Page 99)*

Use the practice for focused breath and noticing thoughts. *(Page 99)*

Use the 4 Ns Strategy: notice, name, normalize, nurture. *(Page 106)*

A

ADVANCEMENT

FOR ACTIVITIES WITH STUDENTS GO TO PAGE 154

Take time to dream. *(Page 136)*

Focus on who you want to become. *(Page 138)*

Write your personal growth oath and repeat it daily. *(Page 142)*

Visualize the result of your growth oath. *(Page 144)*

Choose empowering beliefs. *(Page 146)*

Lower activation energy for healthy rituals. *(Page 152)*

A

MEANING

FOR ACTIVITIES WITH STUDENTS GO TO PAGE 166

Journal about these questions:

- What does life expect of me?
- What is my why?
- How do I bring value to others?

Write your powerful introduction. *(Page 169)*

Take the VIA Character Strengths Survey and reflect on your strengths. *(Page 166)*

What is the story behind why I became a teacher? *(Page 164)*

M

SIX

POSITIVE EMOTIONS

UNLEASHING YOUR BRAIN'S SUPERPOWERS

Positive emotions not only feel good, they also help us learn, grow, and be more resilient.

—Barbara Fredrickson

Harnessing the Power of Authentic Positive Emotions and Befriending Tough Emotions

Positive psychologist Barbara Fredrickson found that people who thrive tend to have at least a three-to-one ratio of positive emotions to difficult emotions. The three-to-one mark is an important tipping point, but we should aim for four to one or five to one.[1] When I share this with people, they'll point out that it's obvious you'll feel great if you experience lots of positive emotions—that's just common sense. But have you noticed how common sense isn't very common? Most Americans are closer to a two-to-one ratio of positive to difficult emotions. Unless you suffer from debilitating anxiety or other clinical conditions, you can decide to generate authentic (not forced) positive emotions throughout your day. Those who thrive understand that it's a choice, that they only have one life to live, and that the time to experience authentic positive emotions is now.

Why do we need a lot more positive emotions than negative ones to thrive? Because positive emotions by their very nature are fleeting, while negative emotions tend to last longer. Our brain has a negativity bias.[2] Think about it: if you receive twenty positive emails and one negative one, what will you spend most of your time focusing on? Or if someone gives you a compliment, how long does the good feeling last before you go back to baseline? Not nearly as long as the bad feeling lasts after a criticism. Luckily, we can train our brains to look for what is right, and we can also intentionally prime and infuse ourselves with positive emotions.

Sometimes people ask me, "Isn't focusing on increasing positive emotions in our lives a luxury for those who have enough money and time?" It's true that if you're constantly threatened or if you're worried about your basic survival, where you'll sleep at night, where you'll get your next meal, and how you'll feed your children, you don't have the opportunity to focus on positive emotions. Barring those conditions, research shows that it is our frame of mind regarding our life situation, rather than our material resources, that determines our experience of positive emotions.[3]

Research has shown a strong correlation between experiencing positive emotions and living longer, having more meaning in life, accepting social support, reporting fewer physical ailments, sleeping better, seeing more possible solutions to problems, and having a greater sense of self efficacy.[4]

One important element to consider with the positivity ratio is that experiencing some negative or difficult emotions is healthy for us. A person who suppresses their negative emotions is a person who is not fully alive, because they end up numbing other emotions as well.[5] Furthermore, when we try to suppress difficult emotions, they usually end up occupying more space. Last, difficult emotions give us important information that we can grow from. We therefore need to employ healthy strategies to welcome difficult emotions and gain resilience.

Before we delve into how to cultivate more positive emotions and deal with difficult ones for ourselves and our students, you should know that experiencing positive emotions profoundly impacts the learning process.

How does experiencing positive emotions tie into effective teaching?

In her research, Barbara Fredrickson found that when people experience positive emotions, they broaden their minds and expand their social, psychological, and intellectual capacities as well as their resilience.

To understand why, think of a difficult emotion, such as fear. Fear narrows and constricts our minds. When we are afraid of something, our attention zeros in on it and everything else is simply not in our awareness. That focus can lead us to experience even more fear, which in turn leads us to narrow and constrict our minds even more, and so on.

Positive emotions have the opposite effect: they widen the array of thoughts, actions, and possibilities that come to mind.[6] They broaden our minds and allow us to consider new possibilities and build new skills. When we experience joy, for example, it can often give us the urge to play, to create, to push the limits of what we think is possible.

Fredrickson's most powerful finding is that positive emotions allow us to become more creative, more collaborative, more curious, and more willing to learn new things. So in effect, when we take time to elicit positive emotions, we are priming our students to learn.

When we take time to elicit positive emotions, we are priming our students to learn.

Anytime I wanted my students to solve a difficult problem or brainstorm topics for group projects, I would first play a game with them (like the ones you can find in this book). As soon as I heard laughter, I knew we were getting to a place where we could start to work.

Since positive emotions are more contagious than difficult ones, spending a few minutes eliciting positive emotions in a group can dramatically shift the energy in a classroom or a staff meeting, even if the energy beforehand was low or tense.

Teachers who experience a healthy positivity ratio in work and life are more likely to try innovative and creative ways to teach. Experiencing a healthy ratio of positive to difficult emotions enhances learning *and* teaching performance.

Experiences That Easily Cultivate Authentic Positive Emotions

Positive emotions come from positive experiences. Since we only have one life to live, it's worth giving some thought to what experiences make you feel truly alive. Be intentional about experiencing these things instead of living life on autopilot.

Incorporate positive experiences into your life deliberately, often, and as soon as possible. Investing in experiences is valuable because they provide us with positive emotions at three different stages: the planning and anticipation stage, the actual experience, and our memories of the experience. Those memories keep paying us a dividend of joy every time we recall the experience. Since our memories stay with us for the rest of our lives, the sooner we experience something positive, the more benefits we'll get.

Once our basic needs are met, investing in positive experiences gives us a lot more fulfillment and satisfaction than getting new things. And many of these experience can be free.

Twenty free or very cheap experiences:
- ► Enjoy a free concert or dance performance at a park in your city or a nearby city
- ► Explore the farmers' market in your city or a nearby city
- ► Visit free (or very cheap) museums or galleries
- ► Stroll around a park and have a picnic

- ► Go to a library and explore new books
- ► Get on a bike or jog around your town
- ► Paint
- ► Go camping
- ► Spend time around a fire pit with friends (or even solo, admiring the fire)
- ► Fly a kite
- ► Tour historic sites in your city or a nearby city
- ► Have a photo shoot of you and a loved one around town
- ► Audit a class at a community college
- ► Join a local meetup
- ► Stargaze
- ► Go for a walk on the beach
- ► Play an instrument
- ► Play music and sing to it (in or out of the shower!)
- ► Take an improv class
- ► Watch a funny stand-up comic (live or online)

WRITING EXERCISE #1: Jot down five experiences that give you a lot of fulfillment. Find at least two free ones, and come up with one or two that may stretch your budget but are still doable. With each experience, account for how much joy you will get from planning for it, doing it, and having the memories of it, then give it a cumulative rating from 1 to 10. Pick the top experience and start planning for it right away. When is the earliest that you can do it? On a scale of 1 to 10, how committed are you to doing it? Is there anything getting in the way? If it's money, the process of saving for an experience can be rewarding in itself. You can see it as a part of the experience.

WRITING EXERCISE #2: What kind of experiences feel like play to you? Do you like playing basketball with others? Drawing by yourself with music in the background? Dancing? Playing board games with others? Write a list of ten activities that you experience as play. Then rank them and answer the following questions about each of the top three.

- What does it feel like when you engage in this activity?
- What do you love the most about it?
- Can you build it into your weekly routine?
- How committed are you to having more of this in your life?

Is there a time and day that you can do it this week? If so, when?

WRITING EXERCISE #3: Experiencing genuine laughter often and consistently can significantly raise your quality of life. Laughter, especially with others, gives us a boost in that moment but also has long-term benefits for our mental health. Jot down three experiences that make you laugh and two people who you laugh a lot with. Is it watching a stand-up comic? A funny sitcom? Does your brother make you laugh? Your kids? Your partner? Write about three ways you could experience more laughter. Commit to doing one this week and have fun with it!

Practices That Cultivate Positive Emotions

One of the most amazing superpowers that we can develop is knowing how to feel positive emotions on command, no matter how mundane or stressful our day is. We can cultivate that ability through the following practices, and in the process, we can rewire our brains to be happier and more resilient.

> One of the most amazing superpowers that we can develop is knowing how to feel positive emotions on command, no matter how mundane or stressful our day is.

Practice #1: Focus on Gratitude

An article from Harvard Health Publishing defines gratitude as "a thankful appreciation for what an individual receives, whether tangible or intangible."[7] When practiced regularly, gratitude deepens relationships, strengthens our immunity, increases optimism, reduces stress, unlocks happiness, and even improves sleep. It can also boost serotonin and dopamine in the brain, which is exactly what antidepressants do.[8]

When we think about what we wish we had, it's easy to develop tunnel vision that leads us to only focus on the negative. When we focus on what we are grateful for, our perspective widens, and we feel more joyful and peaceful. It's impossible to feel grateful and envious or grateful and fearful at the same time.

If we develop a daily practice of finding even one thing that we feel grateful for, we develop and reinforce neural pathways in our brain that make it easier for us to experience gratitude, which reinforces the neural pathway further.[9] Think of the neural pathway as a small creek. The more you practice something, whether it's shooting a basketball, walking, or feeling grateful, the more water flows through that creek. In the beginning it takes a lot of effort, but eventually the small creek turns into a bigger one, and with more reinforcement of the practice, it turns into a river filled with water that has a lot of momentum. Once a neural pathway is well established, it needs less effort to exist. It becomes increasingly easy for us to feel ongoing gratitude, and we become authentically happier.

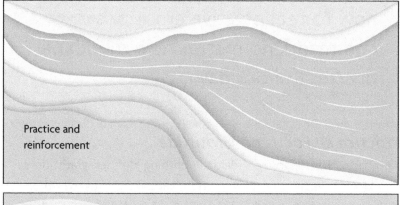

Practice and reinforcement

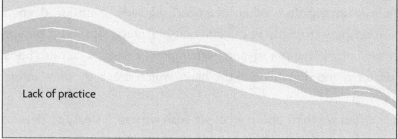

Lack of practice

If you stop practicing for a prolonged period, the neural pathway becomes thinner. That is why it's most helpful to turn the gratitude practice into a ritual.

Have a journal by your bedside table, and right after you get up, write down two things you feel grateful for. Right before you go to sleep, again write down two things. Be consistent for thirty days, and on the last day, journal about what changes you have experienced internally and externally due to this ritual.

Practice #2: Prime Yourself with Positive Imagery (Ideally in the Morning)

In psychology, priming is an occurrence in which exposure to one stimulus influences how a person responds to a subsequent, related stimulus. Psychologist John Bargh conducted a study in which he had participants read words about the elderly, such as *old, wrinkled, retired*, etc.[10] He then timed how long it took them to get from the room to the elevator and compared it to how long it took them to walk that distance before the experiment. They walked significantly slower.

We can use that knowledge to intentionally prime ourselves with positive images and emotions. And if we do so in the morning, it can positively affect our behavior for the rest of the day.

What are the steps to priming for positivity?

STEP 1: Find a quiet place to sit where you can close your eyes and not be disturbed.

STEP 2: (This is optional but highly recommended.) Listen to a playlist of inspirational music.

STEP 3: Think of three things or people that you are grateful for to activate your gratitude muscle.

STEP 4: Visualize yourself moving about your day today feeling happy and peaceful. What do you look like when you are happy and peaceful?

STEP 5: Visualize yourself passionate and excited about taking on your day—the fun stuff and the challenges. Feel the excitement fill you up with energy.

STEP 6: Ask yourself how you are going to be of service to others today and notice how good it feels.

STEP 7: Visualize succeeding at whatever you want to achieve today. How good does that feel?

Allow yourself to feel the feelings, not just think the thoughts, and you will rock your day!

Practice #3: Prime Yourself with Photos That Make You Happy

Print photos of loved ones or experiences that you loved and put them around your house, your class, and/or your office. Initially you'll get a conscious boost of positive emotions from these photos. After a while it will feel as though these photos are just a part of the decor, but on a subconscious level you will still experience positive priming.

Practice #4: Perform Acts of Kindness

Similar to gratitude, acts of kindness toward others, especially if the acts are random, allow us to feel happier and less stressed.[11] You get a sense that you are part of a community and have the capacity to uplift others. Here are some simple (and free) things you can do that will boost your positive emotions and help another person.

- Babysit for a colleague, giving them an unexpected evening off.
- Send a colleague a positive email saying how much you appreciate them and their work.
- Volunteer at the YMCA, a homeless shelter, or an animal shelter.
- Donate clothes that you no longer wear.
- Help a neighbor with a task that requires manual labor.

Practice #5: Go Outside and Connect with Nature

Stepping out into nature or a green space for at least thirty minutes during daylight has a high likelihood of making you feel better,
regardless of how you felt before you went out.[12] This can be particularly powerful in the middle of the day, when many of us need a
little pick-me-up to finish the day strong.

Practice #6: Work Out

Cardiovascular exercise releases healthy hormones and suppresses
stressful hormones, allowing us to feel more calm, happy, and full
of energy.

> **WRITING EXERCISE:** Which practice for cultivating positive emo-
> tions speaks to you the most? Is there a practice (or two) that you
> can turn into a daily ritual? If so, how committed are you to it on
> a scale of 1 to 10? When and where will you do it?

How to Peacefully Allow for Difficult Emotions (Emotional Regulation Tool)

Difficult emotions will arise. Instead of repressing them, we can learn
to welcome them, remembering that all emotions come and go. The
name of the game here is self-regulation practices. Engaging in these
helps us downregulate our nervous system and accept (even welcome) our difficult emotions. Interestingly, the more welcoming we
are of difficult emotions, the faster they pass.

There are a few rules of thumb to remember whenever we experience difficult emotions.

WHEN YOU NAME IT, YOU TAME IT. Identify the emotion by naming it.
For example: "This is anger." As soon as you do that, you become an
observer, and you're not hijacked by the emotion anymore.

YOU ARE NOT YOUR EMOTIONS. Instead of saying "I am sad," say "I feel sad." Our vernacular is important because it's easy to overidentify with difficult emotions.

ALL EMOTIONS CAN BE TRACED TO A SOMATIC SENSATION IN THE BODY. When you notice where you feel an emotion in your body, take a few deep breaths, touch that part of your body with warmth, and invite it to soften every time you exhale. Do this for about sixty seconds.

ALL EMOTIONS ARE TEMPORARY. They always arise and then pass.

THE SOONER YOU CAN BE KIND AND GENTLE WITH YOURSELF, THE SOONER YOU CAN ACCEPT THE DIFFICULT EMOTIONS. Instead of trying to control them, allow yourself to feel these emotions so they can pass.

These rules can help us in our day-to-day lives, but when we struggle with the loss of a loved one, other severe trauma, or clinical depression, the process of managing our emotions is significantly harder and takes longer. The grief of loss can sometimes stay with us forever, and our journey is more about managing the grief when it comes. If this is your case, it is critical to surround yourself with social support and get professional help if you can afford it. You should not go through this alone.

Powerful Practices to Move through Difficult Emotions

You may find that one of these practices works better than another depending on what type of difficult emotions you are feeling. I recommend you try them all.

Practice #1: Self-Compassion Mindfulness Practice

Refer to page 100 for this practice.

Practice #2: The 4 Ns Strategy

Refer to page 106 for this practice.

Practice #3: Welcoming Emotions

In his famous poem "The Guest House,"[13] the prolific poet Jalāl al-Dīn Rumi explains playfully and wisely the benefits that come with welcoming difficult emotions.

The Guest House

> This being human is a guest house.
> Every morning a new arrival.
>
> A joy, a depression, a meanness,
> some momentary awareness comes
> as an unexpected visitor.
>
> Welcome and entertain them all!
> Even if they're a crowd of sorrows,
> who violently sweep your house
> empty of its furniture,
> still, treat each guest honorably.
> He may be clearing you out
> for some new delight.
>
> The dark thought, the shame, the malice,
> meet them at the door laughing,
> and invite them in.
>
> Be grateful for whoever comes,
> because each has been sent
> as a guide from beyond.

Of course, it's easier said than done, especially when you're immersed in these difficult emotions. That's why the simple practice of asking yourself how welcoming you are of these emotions (on a scale of 1 to 10) is a powerful place to start. It's perfectly OK if you're at a 1 or a 2—at least you have more awareness of what you're experiencing. If you find that you are not welcoming your emotions, use this EQ Schools Jedi strategy: Ask yourself, "Can I be welcoming of the fact that I'm not welcoming? And can I be gentle with myself?" Giving yourself permission to not be welcoming now will, paradoxically, lead you to be more welcoming later. After answering those questions, take some deep breaths in and out of your nose, allowing yourself to be exactly as you are. Then check in about how welcoming you feel. If there is movement, great. If not, that's OK. Be welcoming of that, and you'll continue to downregulate.

> Ask yourself, "Can I be welcoming of the fact that I'm not welcoming? And can I be gentle with myself?"

Practice #4: Investigating the Source

Use the QR code or go to eqschools.com/resources to access this resource.

Practice #5: Choosing to Believe That You Live in a Friendly Universe

Use the QR code or go to eqschools.com/resources to access this resource.

Journal Prompts That Elicit Positive Emotions

- Who do you love? Why are they special to you?
- Who loves you? In what ways do they know your love language and show it?
- When did you laugh so hard that your side hurt? Who were you with? Where were you? What, exactly, was so funny?
- What is a moment that you are proud of? (This can be pride in yourself or someone else.)
- What are you looking forward to?
- What is your zen place, where you feel totally relaxed and at peace?
- Write about a moment in your life when you felt totally at peace. Where were you? What were you doing? Who were you with?
- When did you feel passionate, energized, and motivated to get something done? What was the source of your energy?

Journal Prompts That Allow You to Navigate Difficult Emotions with Ease

- Freewrite about what you are feeling and where you feel it in your body. Don't worry about grammar or coming up with solutions. Just write and don't stop writing for at least five minutes.
- How would your best friend talk to you about whatever is triggering these difficult emotions? What would they say?
- If you were your best coach, what would you say to yourself right now?
- We all have an inner child that needs to be nurtured from time to time. Write as if you are nurturing your child and supporting them through the difficult emotions.

- Have a dialogue with your inner child. Write supportive thoughts and hear what they say in response. Then write a response to that. Go back and forth as long as you need.
- Underneath your difficult emotions, what emotion are you trying to avoid? Why? Are you afraid of something? Are you ashamed? Remember to be gentle and honest with yourself in this exploration.
- What are three things that you can do in the next hour that would feel soothing to you?
- Who could you talk to about what you are experiencing? Is there anything stopping you from reaching out for help? Remember that people deeply appreciate it when others are real and vulnerable with them.

Practical Activities for Nurturing Student Positivity and Resilience

When you cultivate a positive environment, you empower the mind to think, innovate, and collaborate.

—Dr. Srikumar Rao

It's easy for students to adopt the "too cool for school" and "life sucks, pass it on" attitude that teenagers (and sometimes even younger kids) can fall into. Below are activities that break those entrenched patterns and infuse students with positive emotions and excitement about learning with others. Speaking from experience, I can tell you that these practices work great on days that students have low energy or come in with a sour mood.

Group/Partner Games

PASS THE SOUND AND MOVEMENT. This game is similar to Pass the Ball, on page 79, but instead of just passing a ball and making a sound, students need to create their own movement and their own sound. It's important that students remember to first mimic the movement and sound that is passed to them. Only then should they create their own sound and movement and pass it to someone else.

I AM A TREE. Students stand in a circle with one student standing in the middle. That student proclaims they are a tree and strikes a tree pose. Then one person from the circle (it can be anyone) comes to the middle and adds to the scene by proclaiming they are something that can be added to the tree. For example, they might say "I'm an apple" and strike an apple pose. Then another person from the circle joins the scene. They might say "I'm a leaf" and strike a leaf pose.

Then the student who started the game decides who will stay in the middle. The first student and the other student rejoin the circle, and the student who gets to stay in the middle must keep their pose and declare again what they are. This starts a new scene. For example, if the student who was an apple stayed in the middle, another student might come in and proclaim they are a sticker. As their pose, they might give the apple student a hug. Then another can come in and proclaim they are a mouth and strike a pose. The student who is an apple will choose who stays in the middle and who rejoins the circle with them. The student in the middle will proclaim what they are again, and the game goes on.

WALK COOL. Use the QR code or go to eqschools.com/resources to access this resource.

Practices, and Exercises That Uplift Students' Well-Being

GRATITUDE CIRCLE. I've done this with students for years, and I've yet to find another exercise that provides them with a window into each other's lives in such a fast, powerful, and lighthearted way.

Tell your students to bring a journal or notebook with them to class every day. As soon as they sit down (before the bell even rings), they are to take out their journal and write down three things or people they feel grateful for. These do not have to be big things. They can be things we usually take for granted, like our health, our bodies, that we have food to eat, or that we live in a peaceful country. When a person writes down what they are grateful for as opposed to just thinking about it, their brain experiences three times the joy.

Encourage your students to take a moment to truly let the gratitude for each thing or person fill them up with joy. Then have students form a circle and each share the most important thing or person they feel grateful for. If you can afford some extra time, have them share why they are grateful for this thing or person.

The key with this gratitude practice is to keep it fresh and to think of new aspects of our lives that we can feel grateful for. On the first day of the week, you can prompt your students to find something they feel grateful for in nature. On the second day, have them think of a friend they are grateful for, etc.

When done consistently, the gratitude circle gives students a window into each other's lives. For a deeper dive on how that happens and how gratitude circles lead to a more equitable classroom environment, use the QR code or go to eqschools.com/resources to access this resource.

A gratitude circle gives students a window into each other's lives

WHAT WENT WELL? I like using this technique sometimes instead of the gratitude circle to change things up a bit. I do it right at the beginning of class, as I've found that this exercise works particularly well when my students need a quick perspective shift.

Once the bell rings, greet your students and ask them to take their notebooks out. Then ask them: "In the last twenty-four hours, what went well for you? It can be something very meaningful, or it can be something very simple. For example, did you have a good conversation with a friend? Did you help your parents with something around the house and they were thankful for that? Did you do well on a test or quiz?"

Because you want your students to relive the experience, tell them to write about it in their journal or notebook with as many details as they can for at least one or two minutes. (If you teach young elementary school students, you can have them draw what happened instead.)

Then ask your students the three questions below and have them journal about those for a few minutes.[14]

1. **Why did it happen?** This is a powerful question because in most cases, students will realize that they made it happen; life doesn't just happen to them. For example, if your student did well on a quiz, they can recognize that it happened because they took time to study. If they had a good conversation with a friend, they put themselves out there and took time to listen and be there for the friend. They develop

a stronger sense of their inner locus of control, recognizing that to a large extent, they are in charge of their lives.

2. **What does it mean to you that it happened?** In some cases, the thing that went well might be mundane, but in other cases, like doing well on a quiz, it can feel incredibly meaningful. Taking a moment to pause and reflect on that can be very uplifting.

3. **How can you have more of this in your life?** In the quiz example, the student might think, "Oh, I did well on the quiz because I actually took time to study. How can I do that again?"

After your students have journaled about these questions, have them think-pair-share their responses.

To see even more benefit, I recommend doing this exercise daily with them for one or two weeks.

RANDOM ACTS OF KINDNESS IN THE CLASSROOM. At the beginning of the week, instruct each student to do a random act of kindness for another student in the class. Tell them that they have two weeks to complete this task. The acts of kindness can be small or big. For example: holding the door for someone as they come in, handing them a pencil when they need one, sharing a cookie with them, helping them study for an upcoming assessment, etc. At the end of the week you could have students share what their act of kindness was and how good it felt to do it.

GRATITUDE LETTER. Use the QR code or go to eqschools.com/resources to access this resource.

For additional activities use the QR code or go to eqschools.com/resources to access this resource.

Emotional Regulation Practices for Students

Many things can trigger difficult emotions in students. Use the practices in the "Awareness" chapter and the regulated breathing practice and script below to support them.

Today we're going to learn about a technique that you can use whenever you feel stressed or worried about anything. It has the potential to lessen any fears or worries you might be experiencing.

To begin, find a comfortable position on your chair with your back straight, the palms of your hands on your legs or your table, and your legs and arms uncrossed. If you are not too tired, close your eyes. Otherwise keep your eyes half open and gaze at the floor. Take a few deep, mindful breaths, in and out, and allow yourself to feel relaxed yet alert.

Now take a moment to notice how your body feels. Does it feel relaxed? Does it feel tense? Is there part of it that feels tighter than usual? Maybe your chest or your shoulders?

Now I'd like you to recall something in your life that brings up some stress for you and perhaps some anxiety. Don't pick anything that is too stressful or leads to too much anxiety. Just pick something that allows you to experience these emotions at a manageable level. It could be studying for a test, talking to a friend about a difficult topic, an upcoming sports game, or talking to your parents about something stressful.

Take a few moments to visualize this experience and notice how your body reacts to it. What sensations do you experience in your body? Does your throat constrict a bit? Is your chest heavier? Do you feel warmer? What else comes up in your body?

Now shift your awareness from your body to your breath, noticing it go in and out for the next few moments.

Now let's practice the technique of regulated breathing. Follow my instructions. We'll be inhaling to the count of four, holding for four, and exhaling to the count of eight.

We'll begin. Inhale, two, three, four. Hold, two, three, four. And exhale, two, three, four, five, six, seven, eight. (Repeat this three more times with your students.)

Now allow your breath to return to its natural speed, and with each breath you take, allow yourself to feel more and more still. In the next few moments, you may choose to go back to regulated breathing or continue to breathe normally

Now take three deep breaths and when you are ready, open your eyes. Check in with your body and notice how you feel.

Reflection Questions:

- How does your body react when you are stressed or worried? What sensations do you feel? In which parts of your body do you feel them?
- What happened when you began to use regulated breathing? How did your body feel before you started using regulated breathing versus after?

RELATIONSHIPS
FOR ACTIVITIES WITH STUDENTS GO TO PAGE 78

Use the pillars of attuned communication: drop in with presence, notice nonverbal cues, get curious, reflect back, empathize, and acknowledge. *(Page 25)*

Name your inference using the three-step method. *(Page 40)*

Respond to students' bids for attention. *(Page 47)*

Use active listening with students when they own the problem. *(Page 58)*

Send an I-message when you own the problem by using the three-step approach. *(Page 63)*

AWARENESS
FOR ACTIVITIES WITH STUDENTS GO TO PAGE 130

Use the practice for regulated breathing. *(Page 99)*

Use the practice for focused breath and noticing thoughts. *(Page 99)*

Use the 4 Ns Strategy: notice, name, normalize, nurture. *(Page 106)*

ADVANCEMENT
FOR ACTIVITIES WITH STUDENTS GO TO PAGE 154

Take time to dream. *(Page 136)*

Focus on who you want to become. *(Page 138)*

Write your personal growth oath and repeat it daily. *(Page 142)*

Visualize the result of your growth oath. *(Page 144)*

Choose empowering beliefs. *(Page 146)*

Lower activation energy for healthy rituals. *(Page 152)*

MEANING
FOR ACTIVITIES WITH STUDENTS GO TO PAGE 166

Journal about these questions:

- What does life expect of me?
- What is my why?
- How do I bring value to others?

Write your powerful introduction. *(Page 169)*

Take the VIA Character Strengths Survey and reflect on your strengths. *(Page 166)*

What is the story behind why I became a teacher? *(Page 164)*

POSITIVE EMOTIONS
FOR ACTIVITIES WITH STUDENTS GO TO PAGE 190

Deliberately infuse positive experiences into your life often and as soon as possible. *(Page 178)*

Have a gratitude practice. *(Page 181)*

Welcome difficult emotions. *(Page 187)*

Prime yourself with positive imagery (ideally in the morning). *(Page 183)*

Choose to believe that you live in a friendly universe. *(Page 188)*

SEVEN

ENERGY MANAGEMENT

THE FOUNDATION OF IT ALL

*Energy, not time, is the fundamental
currency of high performance.*

—Jim Loehr

Supercharge Your Battery:
Adopt Energy Boosters & Seal Energy Leaks

When we are young and have a seemingly endless abundance of energy, we take it for granted. Later, we understand that feeling physically energetic is the foundation for everything we do in life. Without it, life becomes a drag and our RAAMP of well-being begins to tilt downward. When I share this with educators, I often get the following response: "Yes, I should prioritize my energy level." I strongly encourage you to change one word in that sentence. Change your *should* into a *must.* "Yes, I must prioritize my energy level." It's not optional; it's a must. You can't live a joyful, meaningful, and passionate life without it. And you deserve to live an incredible life that is supported by feeling energetic.

Even in my early thirties, I still didn't fully understand that. I remember one day in March, when I was about to start class after pushing it hard all year without many breaks. One of my favorite students of all time looked at me and said, "Mr. Habib, you look like shit." It was said in a compassionate way and the point was beautifully made. She was right. My unbalanced approach had started taking a toll on me physically.

Here is the problem: educators are givers by nature. That is a beautiful thing; however, when we don't balance giving to others with giving to ourselves, we begin to experience burnout and empathy fatigue. We begin to lose ourselves, and in the process, we lose our ability to fully be there for our students. Since most of us are out of practice when it comes to caring for ourselves, we need to understand that it takes time to change our behavior. But with small, consistent rituals, we can begin to map a whole new path for ourselves and for our students.

One of the best places to start is by changing our mindset about energy management. This is not a topic you learn about in teacher prep programs, but if you've taught for more than a year, you know it should be.

Teaching is a marathon, so it's helpful to assume the mindset of an athlete when it comes to managing our energy. Athletes understand that to reach peak performance, rest is just as important as practice.[1] They believe that the correct type of rest is a part of their work. I believe every educator should know that when they are resting properly, they are fulfilling a part of their work. Why? Because proper rest allows them to be at their best when they are teaching and supporting students. This is not just a sweet sentiment. It's an empirical truth that unfortunately too many educators and administrators don't understand, don't believe in, or are not committed to. If you consistently approach the world on an empty tank, not only do you suffer but those around you do too.

Think of the common scenario of a mother coming home cranky after a long day of work. Her kids want her immediate attention, but she knows that if she takes thirty minutes to work out on the elliptical machine, she will feel a lot better and be a much kinder and more energetic parent. Taking time to work out on the elliptical machine is a seemingly selfish act, but it's serving the whole family in the most self-less way possible. Being focused on yourself at times does not make you self-centered; rather, it allows you to be at your best for those you love.

> **WRITING EXERCISE:** Journal about the following questions:
> - In what ways has society taught you that investing in your self-care is selfish?
> - Where did you first hear this message? From your parents? A sibling? A friend? A coworker?
> - List three reasons why their rationale is faulty.

The Importance of Recovery Periods

According to Tal Ben-Shahar, stress is not in itself a problem. Stress can help us grow in important ways, making us ready to take on new challenges. Too much stress is bad, of course, but it's usually not the amount of stress that leads people to get sick or burn out—it's the duration of the stress. Stress without recovery is the problem.

Stress without recovery is the problem.

Ben-Shahar makes that point clear by reminding us that when we go to the gym and lift weights, we stress our muscles. But then we take a break, and only after our muscles rest for some time do we come back and stress them again. It's the combination of work *and* rest that allows our muscles to build. If we were to go to the gym and stress our muscles without taking a break, we would experience a physical injury. The same is true mentally and emotionally. Without recovery periods, we injure ourselves, we get sick, and at the very least, we get burned out. The same is true, of course, for our students.

How to Rest

The key with rest is to nourish your body, your mind, and your soul. Any activity that allows you to do all three will replenish your battery. But it's important to make sure that, first and foremost, your body gets nourished. Here are ten activities to try:

- Dance to your favorite song (even if you're alone)
- Go for a mindful walk outside and notice nature all around you
- Work out for thirty minutes (or longer)
- Take a fifteen-minute nap
- Garden
- Read a book
- Play with or pet your cat or dog
- Mindfully wash dishes with warm water
- Take a bath
- Play an instrument

> **WRITING EXERCISE:** Make a list of ten activities that nourish your body, mind, and soul. Then pick your top three and decide when you will engage in each of them in the next two days. Pick a specific time and place to do so. Then write this commitment down in your journal to help you follow through.

When to Rest

A lot of research shows that we need to give ourselves three levels of recovery period.

1. Every ninety minutes of work, give yourself a fifteen-minute break.[2]

2. Every week, take one intentional day off.

3. Every year, go on a vacation for at least a week (ideally).

The 90/15 Rule

When you give yourself fifteen minutes of recovery after ninety minutes of work, you will be more efficient, creative, and productive in your next ninety minutes of work. Most importantly, you'll also be able to more easily handle any stress that comes your way. For one week, set a timer for ninety-minute periods throughout your working day. This will make you more likely to take breaks on time.

WRITING EXERCISE: Visualize your fifteen minutes of recovery for every ninety minutes of work. If fifteen minutes is too hard for you to imagine (after all, you are an educator), can you give yourself ten minutes? Can you give yourself five minutes? If your answer is "No, because I have to teach," well, guess who else needs that recovery period? Your students! So how can you incorporate a recovery period for them as well?

Take five minutes to visualize what short recovery breaks can look like throughout the day when you're not teaching. Then visualize what those breaks look like in your classroom. Does everyone take a mini nap? Or a stretch break? Does everyone dance to music? Or run through a somatic mindfulness practice?

After your visualization, journal about the following:

- What felt good about this visualization?
- What recovery periods are you willing to commit to for a week?
- What might get in the way of staying consistent?
- What benefits would you and your students get from these recovery periods?

Intentional Day Off

The fourth of the Ten Commandments is "Remember the Sabbath day, to keep it holy." Practicing Jews around the world are *commanded* to rest on the seventh day of the week. In other words, it isn't a choice. And there is great wisdom in making it a commandment—not optional. Because when we have full freedom to do whatever we want with our time, paradoxically, most of us choose to work or engage in activities that are not restful. The structure of the Jewish law provides real freedom and real balance.

When I share that research shows having one day a week for rest is paramount for your resilience and well-being, people often tell me, "Roni, I actually have two days to rest! I have the weekend." Your weekend is like your garage. If you are not intentional about it, you just fill it up with shit.

If it's easier for you to have your day off on Sunday, that's great. And if you can't give yourself a full day of rest, can you give yourself five hours? To be clear, rest doesn't mean that you're lying in bed all day. Doing yoga, going for a walk, or even playing with your kids can be a part of your rest routine, as long as these activities nourish your body and recharge your batteries.

WRITING EXERCISE: Create a Sabbath for yourself. Pick one day of the week when you'll spend the whole day resting without looking at screens.
- What day will it be?
- When will you get up?
- What activities will you do?
- If you like taking a nap, when will you do that?
- How will you draw boundaries to ensure that this time is protected?
- How will doing this make you more productive the rest of the week?

Your weekend is like your garage. If you are not intentional about it, you just fill it up with shit.

- On a scale of 1 to 10, how committed are you to doing this every week for one month?
- If you are not at 8, 9, or 10, what's getting in the way?

The Week-Off Rule

In Europe people often take four to five weeks off work every year. Many Americans who have jobs that offer two weeks of vacation don't even take advantage of that entire time off. This is because they feel guilty doing so when their coworkers seem to work more than they do. Luckily for us educators, we have the summer! Yet it's still hard for some of us to block off one or two weeks for complete rest and leisure. Given all the research-proven benefits of rest, not taking time off is an irrational mistake.

I'm aware that not everyone can afford to go on a trip, and I'm not suggesting your vacation has to be expensive. It can be a simple staycation at home where you get to do whatever you want. And if you have kids, carve out time to play with them as well as time away from them (get a friend to help you if need be).

WRITING EXERCISE: Journal about the following prompts:
- If you didn't have to worry about money, what kind of vacation would you go on?
- How long would you go for? Dream big. (Four to six weeks is a great answer!)
- What types of activities would you do?
- What would be the most exciting and rejuvenating parts?
- How could you experience some of that same excitement and rejuvenation within your actual budget?
- What would a vacation within your budget look like? (Keep the same expansive mindset as before.)
- When will you go on it?
- On a scale of 1 to 10, how committed are you to going?
- If you're not at 8, 9, or 10, what's stopping you?

Plugging Our Deepest Energy Drain

We all experience things in life that can drain our energy. Working overtime, dealing with difficult people, adapting to new circumstances, etc. Yet one of the biggest energy drains occurs under the surface. It's called worrying, and most of the time, we worry about things that are out of our control.

Think about one thing in your life that you worry about. Now think about what part of it you have control over and what part of it you don't. Instead of worrying about the part you do have control over, make a plan to respond to it in the best way you can. What would that look like? When can you start taking actionable steps toward shifting the part that you do have control over? Is it today? Is it this week? Even taking a small step today can start momentum and make a huge difference down the line.

Next, recognize what you don't have control over and truly let it go. You can achieve this by doing your best to welcome any difficult emotions (including helplessness) that arise as a result of you not having control of this situation. Then decide to truly let it go and stick to your decision.

Recognize what you don't have control over and truly let it go.

WRITING EXERCISE: Recall something that worries you and freewrite about it for a few minutes. Then answer the following questions:

- What part do you have control over?
- What plan can you make to address the part that you have control over?
- When can you start implementing that plan?
- What part of it do you not have control over?
- On a scale of 1 to 10, how welcoming are you of the helplessness that you feel? If you are not welcoming, can you welcome that you are not welcoming?
- Are you ready to let that part go? Why or why not?
- Is there a fear that comes up for you? If so, what is it? Is your worst fear realistic? What kind of support do you need to let it go?

On the face of it, energy management and regeneration is simple: increase your energy givers (recovery periods) and decrease your energy drainers (worrying, beating yourself up, holding on to anger, etc.). To experience energy regeneration, however, we need to change our behavior, which can be challenging. Remember that it's a process. You'll see immediate results as you implement the exercises in this chapter, but these are temporary; it will take more time to experience a sustained increase in energy level. That's OK. Remember to be patient with yourself during your journey, and if you fall off the wagon one day, don't beat yourself up—simply recommit to energy regeneration. You, your loved ones, and your students deserve it.

Journal Prompts to Manage and Regenerate Energy

- On a scale of 1 to 10, how satisfied am I with my level of energy in the morning? Afternoon? Evening?
- What activities energize me? Why am I not doing them more often? How can I build them into my life?
- What can I do to get great sleep consistently?
- What would my life look and feel like if I didn't worry at all? How would my body feel?
- Which people in my life give me energy? How can I spend more time with them?
- Which people sap my energy? How can I love these people from afar?

Fun Activities to Energize Students

I loved using the activities below in March and toward the end of October. Those were the times when I found "new year" energy had waned for students. These activities boosted my students' energy right away.

Group Rock Paper Scissors

Pair students up and tell them to play one game of rock paper scissors. The winner gets to duel with a winner from another pair. The loser becomes the most amazing and loud cheerleader for the winner, shouting their names and encouraging them to beat their next opponent. After the next round, the winner will have three cheerleaders behind them as they duel another second-round winner. The game continues until there is just one winner left.

Emphasize that the support, enthusiasm, and team effort from the cheerleaders is way more important than winning.

Dance Clapping

Participants are in pairs for this game. They will stand up and face each other. They are to move their arms to a beat. Each participant can move both their arms up, to the right, or to the left. If partners move their arms in different directions, they gently slap their own thighs on the next beat. Then they again move their arms up, left, or right. If partners move their arms in the same direction, they slap their own thighs, and on the next beat they give each other high fives with both hands. Then they slap their own thighs again, and on the next beat they move their arms up, left, or right. Play this game for about two minutes. For an instructional video clip, use the QR code or go to eqschools.com/resources.

Rapid-Fire Storytelling Relay

Divide students into two or three equal teams and have each group form a line. Choose a random topic for a story, such as "a dinner with Darth Vader" or "aliens invade earth." Or have students come up with a school-appropriate topic. All teams are going to use the same topic. The first student in line starts their team's story with a single sentence. After completing the sentence, the student moves to the end of the line. The second student in line quickly adds another sentence that flows smoothly from the previous one, and then they move to the end of the line. The process continues for three to five minutes. At the end of the game, each group recaps their story to the whole class.

Stretch Drill Sergeant

Use the QR code or go to eqschools.com/resources to access this resource.

R

RELATIONSHIPS

**FOR ACTIVITIES WITH STUDENTS,
GO TO PAGE 78**

Use the pillars of attuned communication: drop in with presence, notice nonverbal cues, get curious, reflect back, empathize, and acknowledge. *(Page 25)*

Name your inference using the three-step method. *(Page 40)*

Respond to students' bids for attention. *(Page 47)*

Use active listening with students when they own the problem. *(Page 58)*

Send an I-message when you own the problem by using the three-step approach. *(Page 63)*

A

AWARENESS

**FOR ACTIVITIES WITH STUDENTS,
GO TO PAGE 130**

Use the practice for regulated breathing. *(Page 99)*

Use the practice for focused breath and noticing thoughts. *(Page 99)*

Use the 4 Ns Strategy: notice, name, normalize, nurture. *(Page 106)*

E N E R G Y

List recovery activities.
(Page 201)

Implement the 90/15 rule.
(Page 202)

A   M   P

ADVANCEMENT

FOR ACTIVITIES WITH STUDENTS, GO TO PAGE 154

Take time to dream. *(Page 136)*

Focus on who you want to become. *(Page 138)*

Write your personal growth oath and repeat it daily. *(Page 142)*

Visualize the result of your growth oath. *(Page 144)*

Choose empowering beliefs. *(Page 146)*

Lower activation energy for healthy rituals. *(Page 152)*

MEANING

FOR ACTIVITIES WITH STUDENTS, GO TO PAGE 166

Journal about these questions:

- What does life expect of me?
- What is my why?
- How do I bring value to others?

Write your powerful introduction. *(Page 169)*

Take the VIA Character Strengths Survey and reflect on your strengths. *(Page 166)*

What is the story behind why I became a teacher? *(Page 164)*

POSITIVE EMOTIONS

FOR ACTIVITIES WITH STUDENTS, GO TO PAGE 190

Deliberately infuse positive experiences into your life often and as soon as possible. *(Page 178)*

Have a gratitude practice. *(Page 181)*

Welcome difficult emotions. *(Page 187)*

Prime yourself with positive imagery (ideally in the morning). *(Page 183)*

Choose to believe that you live in a friendly universe. *(Page 188)*

MANAGEMENT

FOR ACTIVITIES WITH STUDENTS, GO TO PAGE 208

Implement the Sabbath rule. *(Page 203)*

Plug the energy drain of worry. *(Page 207)*

EIGHT

THE COURAGE TO TEACH AND TO WALK THE WALK

Children learn more from what you are than what you teach.

—W. E. B. Du Bois

It Takes Courage

It takes courage to build deeper connections in the classroom and prioritize your students' well-being, especially if you've never carved out time for this during class before. It's particularly scary if your colleagues are not doing this with their classes.

I want to share a secret with you. I've worked with over one hundred schools, and every principal, superintendent, or other administrator in those schools has told me something to this effect: "Roni, I want my teachers to prioritize joy, relationships, fun, and emotional connections in the classroom, but they are so in the habit of meeting academic standards and dealing with the stress surrounding teaching that they don't believe I want them to prioritize their students' and their own well-being. It's as though I have to give them permission to focus on it." I've heard this message over and over again. My point is that you're not only likely to be safe incorporating RAAMP strategies into your classroom—you'll be celebrated.

You're not only likely to be safe incorporating RAAMP strategies into your classroom—you'll be celebrated.

To get in touch with your courage, it's valuable to tune into your *why*. Why do you teach? If your answer is "I teach because I get joy from seeing students read for the first time," I completely understand, and I think that's a beautiful reason to teach. Yet I encourage you to dig deeper and ask yourself why you care about that. When you come up with an answer, ask yourself why you care about *that* and so on. You'll likely find that at the bottom of it all, you teach because you care about the well-being of your students first and foremost.

Let's take the above example: "I teach because I get joy out of seeing students read for the first time." Why do you care about that? "Because reading is a vital skill that kids must have to be successful in school and in life." Why do you care about that? "Because I want them to be successful in school and in life." And why is that important? "Because I want them to have the best chance to lead the life they want and to be a contributing member of our society." Why is that important to you? "Because that can lead them to live a happy, fulfilling life."

It can feel silly to keep asking ourselves the *why* question almost like a toddler would ask a parent. But a lot of wisdom can come from slowing down and recognizing what's at the root of our teaching purpose. I'm willing to bet a lot of money that if you do this exercise, you'll get to an answer that in one way or another points to optimizing your students' well-being, resilience, fulfillment, or joy in life. So instead of going about it in a circuitous way, incorporate RAAMP directly and overtly into your time with your students.

> Instead of going about it in a circuitous way, incorporate RAAMP directly and overtly into your time with your students.

Walk the Walk

A woman in India told her son to stop eating so much sugar. The boy didn't listen and kept eating as many sweets as he wanted. The mother said it again, but the boy didn't stop. Exasperated, the mother told the boy that if he didn't stop eating so much sugar, she would take him to Mahatma Gandhi, who would tell him to stop. The boy didn't believe she would follow through with it and kept eating sweets. To his surprise, the mother told him to pack his bags one morning and get ready for the long journey to Gandhi's ashram.

When they finally got to the ashram, they waited in line for hours before being allowed into Gandhi's room. Once it was time for them to enter, the mother said, "Mahatma, thank you so much for seeing us. My son is eating way too many sweets. I told him to stop eating so much sugar, but he won't listen to me. I brought him here because I know that he will listen to you. Will you please tell him to stop eating so much sugar?"

Gandhi looked at the boy and then looked back at the mother and said, "Ma'am, please come back with the boy in one month." The mother was surprised and disappointed, but it was Gandhi, and you did what he said.

The next month, her son was still eating too much sugar, so they went back to the ashram. As they walked into the room, she said, "Mahatma, we were here a month ago . . ."

Gandhi replied, "Yes, of course, I remember you. Is your son still eating too much sugar?"

The mother replied, "Yes! He still is. He is not listening to me, but he will listen to you. Can you please tell him to stop eating so much sugar?"

Gandhi looked at the boy and said, "Son, stop eating so much sugar."

The mother was very thankful, but she couldn't help but ask Gandhi, "Mahatma, why didn't you say this to my son a month ago? It's only six words and we had to wait a month to hear them."

Gandhi responded, "It's because a month ago, I was eating too much sugar."

When Gandhi said, "You have to be the change you wish to see in the world," he meant it. Talk only goes so far. Action speaks way louder.

The most important ingredient in students' learning experience is not the room they are taught in, other students in the class, or even the type of pedagogy followed (though that last one is definitely important). The most important ingredient is simply the human being who teaches them. Is the teacher excited to be there? Is she energetic enough to meet the energy of the kids? Is he feeling optimistic about his impact as an educator? Does he have tools to help himself when he doubts he's making a difference in his students' lives? Is she in a state of mind that allows her to be creative and excited about teaching? Does he believe in himself? Does he believe in his students? Does she have the inner resources to meet her students with a genuine and caring smile? Does he have the communication tools to connect with his students?

Our students can pick up on our energy and our emotions. While it's easy to teach them about RAAMP, the importance of creating routines to feel positive emotions, and how to welcome difficult emotions, none of that will stick if they don't see the adult in front of them actually living by those ideals. I can't tell you how many times I've seen well-meaning teachers yell at kids to be mindful!

If you are truly in the business of changing other people's lives, you need to start with your own. That means cultivating healthy habits such as mindfulness practices, workouts, journaling, and taking time to deeply connect and laugh with others. When you commit to experiencing more RAAMP in your life and you follow through, your students will learn from you seamlessly and genuinely. They'll see you regulating yourself with breathing exercises instead of reacting to disruptions with anger. You'll show them how you develop your growth mindset by choosing empowering beliefs, and they'll see how these beliefs allow you try new ways of teaching while being completely fine with failing. You can demonstrate how you learn from and celebrate your failures. If you're passionate about life, resilient, and peaceful (and kind to yourself when you're not), your energy will rub off on your students and they will be primed to learn from and with you.

The lessons, practices, and skills of RAAMP will undoubtedly help you at work. But they have an even more essential purpose. While your job is super important (I would say it's the most important job out there), it's not as important as your health, your well-being, and your ability to live life to the fullest. Your RAAMP will support you to live that life. I invite you to choose this path for yourself. You deserve all of that and more.

NOTES

Chapter One

1 Felicia A. Huppert, "Psychological Well-Being: Evidence Regarding Its Causes and Consequences," *Applied Psychology: Health and Well-Being* 1, no. 2 (July 1, 2009): 137–64, https://doi.org/10.1111/j.1758 -0854.2009.01008.x.

2 Seph Fontane Pennock, "The Hedonic Treadmill: Are We Forever Chasing Rainbows?," Positive Psychology, modified April 19, 2023, https:// positivepsychology.com/hedonic-treadmill/.

3 Sonja Lyubomirsky, *The How of Happiness: A New Approach to Getting the Life You Want* (New York: Penguin Press, 2008), 62.

4 Cary Cherniss, "Emotional Intelligence: What It Is and Why It Matters," Consortium for Research on Emotional Intelligence in Organizations, April 15, 2000, https://www.eiconsortium.org/reports/what_is_ emotional_intelligence.html.

5 Bronnie Ware, "The Top Five Regrets of the Dying," *Bronnie Ware* (blog), accessed February 10, 2023, https://bronnieware.com/blog/ regrets-of-the-dying/.

Chapter Two

1 Elizabeth Hopper, "Maslow's Hierarchy of Needs Explained," ThoughtCo., updated February 24, 2020, https://www.thoughtco.com/ maslows-hierarchy-of-needs-4582571.

2 "What Is Bloom's Taxonomy?," Bloom's Taxonomy, accessed February 10, 2023, https://bloomstaxonomy.net/.

3 Annie McKee, "The Science Behind Shared Emotions and the Benefits of Laughter at Work," Annie McKee, July 31, 2018, http://www. anniemckee.com/science-behind-shared-emotions-benefits-laughter -work/.

4 Daniel Goleman, Richard Boyatzis, and Annie McKee, *Primal Leadership: Realizing the Power of Emotional Intelligence* (Boston: Harvard Business Review Press, 2002), 22.

5 Ibid.

6   Shawn Achor, *The Happiness Advantage: The Seven Principles of Positive Psychology That Fuel Success and Performance at Work* (New York: Crown Business, 2010), 44.

7   "How Much of Communication Is Nonverbal?," The University of Texas Permian Basin (blog), accessed February 10, 2023, https://online.utpb.edu/about-us/articles/communication/how-much-of-communication-is-nonverbal/.

8   Jane Taylor, "The Four Attributes of Empathy," Habits for Wellbeing, accessed February 10, 2023, https://www.habitsforwellbeing.com/the-four-attributes-of-empathy/.

9   Adam Grant, "The Science of Productive Conflict," April 13, 2021, *WorkLife with Adam Grant*, TED podcast transcript, website, 39:55, https://www.ted.com/podcasts/worklife/the-science-of-productive-conflict-transcript.

10 Zach Brittle, "Turn Towards Instead of Away," The Gottman Institute (blog), accessed February 10, 2023, https://www.gottman.com/blog/turn-toward-instead-of-away/.

11 Christopher Dollard, "Invest in Your Relationship: The Emotional Bank Account," The Gottman Institute (blog), accessed February 10, 2023, https://www.gottman.com/blog/invest-relationship-emotional-bank-account/.

12 Shruti S. Poulsen, "A Fine Balance: The Magic Ratio to a Healthy Relationship," Purdue University Extension, Consumer and Family Sciences, accessed February 10, 2023, https://www.extension.purdue.edu/extmedia/cfs/cfs-744-w.pdf.

13 Barbara Fredrickson, *Positivity* (New York: Crown Publishers, 2009), 124.

14 Thomas Gordon, *T.E.T.: Teacher Effectiveness Training* (New York: P.H. Hyden, 1974).

15 Mudita Nisker and Dan Clurman, *Let's Talk: An Essential Guide to Skillful Communication* (San Francisco: Let's Talk Method, 2022), 44.

Chapter Three

1   Krista Tippet, "Ellen Langer, Science of Mindlessness and Mindfulness," On Being (podcast), November 2, 2017, https://onbeing.org/programs/ellen-langer-science-of-mindlessness-and-mindfulness-nov2017/.

2   Viktor E. Frankl, *Man's Search for Meaning* (Boston: Beacon Press, 1959), 65.

3   Kirk Warren Brown and Richard M. Ryan, "The Benefits of Being Present: Mindfulness and Its Role in Psychological Well-Being," Public Library of Science (PLOS), accessed February 10, 2023, https://pubmed.ncbi.nlm.nih.gov/12703651/.

4   Shawn Achor, *The Happiness Advantage: The Seven Principles of Positive Psychology That Fuel Success and Performance at Work* (New York: Crown Business, 2010), 122.

5   "Checklist of Cognitive Distortions," Arkansas Families First, accessed February 10, 2023, https://arfamiliesfirst.com/wp-content/uploads/2013/05/Cognitive-Distortions.pdf.

6   John Kabat-Zinn, *Full Catastrophe Living: Using the Wisdom of Your Body and Mind to Face Stress, Pain, and Illness* (New York: Random House, 2009), 277.

7   Tara Brach, *Radical Acceptance: Embracing Your Life with the Heart of a Buddha* (New York: Bantam Books, 2003), 27.

8   Ibid., 28.

9   Krista Tippet, "Ellen Langer, Science of Mindlessness and Mindfulness," On Being (podcast) November 2, 2017, https://onbeing.org/programs/ellen-langer-science-of-mindlessness-and-mindfulness-nov2017/.

10   "Implementation Intentions," iResearchNet, accessed February 10, 2023, http://psychology.iresearchnet.com/social-psychology/control/implementation-intentions/.

11   Kristin Neff, "Exercise 2: Self Compassion Break," Self-Compassion.org, accessed June 22, 2023. https://self-compassion.org/exercise-2-self-compassion-break/.

12   Lauri Nummenmaa, Enrico Glerean, Riita Hari, and Jari K. Hietanen, "Bodily Maps of Emotions," *Journal of Cognitive Neuroscience* 111, 2: 646–51, https://www.pnas.org/doi/10.1073/pnas.1321664111.

13   Bruce Freeman, "Name It to Tame It: Labelling Emotions to Reduce Stress & Anxiety," Oral Health, May 3, 2021, https://www.oralhealthgroup.com/features/name-it-to-tame-it-labelling-emotions-to-reduce-stress-anxiety/.

14   Roderik J. S. Gerritsen and Guido P. H. Band, "Breath of Life: The Respiratory Vagal Stimulation Model of Contemplative Activity," National Center for Biotechnology Information, accessed February 10, 2023, https://www.ncbi.nlm.nih.gov/pmc/articles/PMC6189422/.

15   Doc Childre, Howard Martin, Deborah Rozman, and Rollin McCraty, *Heart Intelligence: Connecting with the Intuitive Guidance of the Heart,* (New York, New York: Waterfront Press, 2022), 82.

---

16 Byron Katie, "Judge Your Neighbor Worksheet," 2019, accessed June 2023, https://thework.com/wp-content/uploads/2019/02/jyn_en_mod_6feb2019_r4_form1.pdf.

Chapter Four

1 James Clear, *Atomic Habits: An Easy & Proven Way to Build Good Habits & Break Bad Ones* (New York: Penguin Random House, 2018), 32.

2 Wray Herbert, "How Beliefs about the Self Shape Personality and Behavior," Association for Psychological Science, August 1, 2007, https://www.psychologicalscience.org/observer/how-beliefs-about-the-self-shape-personality-and-behavior.

3 Tim Blankert and Melvyn R. W. Hamstra, "Imagining Success: Multiple Achievement Goals and the Effectiveness of Imagery," National Center for Biotechnology Information, accessed February 10, 2023, https://www.ncbi.nlm.nih.gov/pmc/articles/PMC5351796/.

4 Shawn Achor, *The Happiness Advantage: The Seven Principles of Positive Psychology That Fuel Success and Performance at Work* (New York: Crown Business, 2010), 156.

5 Carol Dweck, *Mindset: The New Psychology of Success* (New York: Random House, 2007), 6.

Chapter Five

1 Viktor E. Frankl, *Man's Search for Meaning* (Boston: Beacon Press, 1959), 76.

2 Ibid.

3 Margaret L. Kern and Michael L. Wehmeyer, eds., *The Palgrave Handbook of Positive Education* (London: Palgrave Macmillan, 2021), 558.

4 Frank Martela and Michael F. Steger, "The Three Meanings of Meaning in Life: Distinguishing Coherence, Purpose, and Significance," *Journal of Positive Psychology* 11, no. 5 (2016): 531–45; Login S. George and Crystal L. Park, "Meaning in Life as Comprehension, Purpose, and Mattering: Toward Integration and New Research Questions," *Review of General Psychology* 20, no. 3 (2016): 205–20.

5 "The 24 Character Strengths," VIA Institute on Character, accessed February 10, 2023, https://www.viacharacter.org/character-strengths.

6 "Questionnaire Center," Authentic Happiness, University of Pennsylvania, accessed February 10, 2023, https://www.authentichappiness.sas.upenn.edu/testcenter.

7 Tal Ben-Shahar, *Happier: Learn the Secrets to Daily Joy and Lasting Fulfillment* (New York: McGraw-Hill, 2007), 72.

8 Christopher Peterson, *A Primer in Positive Psychology* (New York: Oxford University Press, 2006), 99.

Chapter Six

1 Barbara Fredrickson, *Positivity* (New York: Crown Publishers, 2009), 32.

2 Jill Suttie, "How to Overcome Your Brain's Fixation on Bad Things," *Greater Good Magazine*, January 13, 2020, https://greatergood.berkeley .edu/article/itemhow_to_overcome_your_brains_fixation_on_bad _things.

3 Barbara Fredrickson, *Positivity* (New York: Crown Publishers, 2009), 154.

4 Michael A. Cohn et al., "Happiness Unpacked: Positive Emotions Increase Life Satisfaction by Building Resilience," National Center for Biotechnology Information, accessed February 10, 2023, https://www. ncbi.nlm.nih.gov/pmc/articles/PMC3126102/.

5 Hanan Parvez, "Emotional Suppression: Causes and Consequences," Psych Mechanics, updated June 13, 2022, https://www. psychmechanics.com/effects-of-suppressing-your-emotions/.

6 Barbara Fredrickson, *Positivity* (New York: Crown Publishers, 2009), 55.

7 "Giving Thanks Can Make You Happier," Harvard Health Publishing, August 14, 2021, https://www.health.harvard.edu/healthbeat/ giving-thanks-can-make-you-happier.

8 Madhuleena Roy Chowdhury, "The Neuroscience of Gratitude and Effects on the Brain," Positive Psychology, April 9, 2019, https:// positivepsychology.com/neuroscience-of-gratitude/.

9 "Neuroplasticity," Physiopedia, accessed February 10, 2023, https:// www.physio-pedia.com/Neuroplasticity.

10 John A. Bargh, "What Have We Been Priming All These Years? On the Development, Mechanisms, and Ecology of Nonconscious Social Behavior," National Center for Biotechnology Information, accessed February 10, 2023, https://www.ncbi.nlm.nih.gov/pmc/articles/ PMC2763379/.

11 Sonja Lyubomirsky, *The How of Happiness: A New Approach to Getting the Life You Want* (New York: Penguin Press, 2008), 283.

12 Chantelle Pattemore, "Spending Time in Nature Is Good for You: New Research Explains Why," Healthline, August 5, 2022, https:// www.healthline.com/health-news/spending-time-in-nature-is-goo d-for-you-new-research-explains-why.

13 Coleman Barks, *The Essential Rumi: A Poetry Anthology* (reissue, San Francisco Harper. 1995), 108–109.

14 Christopher Peterson, *A Primer in Positive Psychology* (New York: Oxford University Press, 2006), 38.

Chapter Seven

1   Rick Ansorge, "Rest and Recovery Are Critical for an Athlete's Physiological and Psychological Well-Being," UC Health Today, February 7, 2022, https://www.uchealth.org/today/rest-and-recovery-for -athletes-physiological-psychological-well-being/.

2   Tony Schwartz, "The 90-minute solution: How Building In Periods of Renewal Can Change Your Work and Your Life," HuffPost, December 6, 2017, accessed June 22, 2023, https://www.huffpost.com/entry/ work-life-balance-the-90_b_578671?ref=buffer.com.

ACKNOWLEDGMENTS

This book would not have been written without the unwavering support of my dear friend and writing mentor, Tarn Wilson. Tarn is an author, a master teacher, a coach of teachers, and one of the most generous people that I've ever come across. Her wisdom, expertise, and positive energy provided me with the spark that I needed in order to keep writing and to get this book out into the world. She has met with me on countless mornings for our writing sessions, provided me with powerful ideas for the book, edited parts of the book, and held me in my excitement, fear, and all the emotions in between as I wrote this book. I will cherish those gifts, and our friendship, forever.

In the process of writing the book, I reached out to a select group of educators and leaders to receive feedback and to make sure that what I wrote in this book didn't sound crazy. Each educator on this list is an absolute genius in the craft of educating students and in leading schools. Each of them is also a gem of a person. A huge thanks goes out to Sean Healy, Susana Herrera, James Parker, Lisa Highfill, Elizabeth Matchett, Nicole Steward, Wade Spenader, Martin Blank, and Rushton Hurley. Thank you for your time, energy, and wise words.

I'm amazed by Jenny Munro's magical editing abilities and deeply grateful for her altruism as she voluntarily edited the book, tightened the text, and provided suggestions that strengthened the work, all in one week.

To my publisher, Dave Burgess: I'm deeply grateful for your belief in me, your support, your ability to show me when something needed more work and coach me through it, and your amazing talent at helping me share my message succinctly and powerfully. A big thanks goes to Tara Martin, who helped me take the book from a first draft to an actual book and who shined positive energy on me and the book every step along the way. And to Salvatore Borriello who spent countless hours with his team editing the book and teaching me how to become a professional writer—thank you, Sal!

To the teachers in my life, such as Frank Andrews, who have had such a profound impact on who I am as a person and educator and who introduced me to many of the concepts in this book, a big heart-felt thank you.

To my students, who taught me the most about what it means to be a great teacher and who made teaching so fun for so many years, I'm deeply thankful.

Thanks go to my brothers, Nathan and David Habib, who remind me to not take my work too seriously, who I can laugh with until my side hurts, and whose unconditional love is always a phone call away.

Thanks also to Owen Ward for being the kind of friend who shows up, who listens, who can lift me up when I'm down, challenge me when I need to grow, and who I can have a blast with.

A special thank you goes to my girlfriend, Randee Schwartz, who reminds me regularly that my work is a mitzvah, who is always there for me when doubts creep in, whose sense of humor brightens my world, and whose huge heart provides me with joy and comfort. Thank you for leading me into the wonderful world of yoga, for being my rock, for the opportunity to grow together, and for all the incredibly fun adventures that keep charging my battery.

And thanks to everyone else who has read, listened, and supported me in this process.

Lastly, and most importantly, I'm deeply grateful for my kids. Eli and Leah: You give me so much joy daily and remind me everyday of what is actually most important in life.

ABOUT THE AUTHOR

RONI HABIB is a speaker, author, and expert in helping leaders, educators, and parents become happier, more resilient, more connected to their purpose, and more playful. The founder of EQ Schools, he speaks and leads workshops in organizations nationally and abroad. His dynamic keynotes leave audiences laughing, insightful, elevated, and inspired to take action.

Early in his career, Roni struggled with the high stresses and demands of teaching, even losing touch with why he wanted to be a teacher in the first place. It was so painful that he finally discovered the power of integrating improv, mindfulness, emotional intelligence, and positive psychology in his own life as well as at work. Soon, he felt called to share this new approach with the world.

In the last decade with EQ Schools, Roni has taught and inspired thousands of teachers, principals, superintendents, administrators, business leaders, and parents.

Prior to earning his master of education and teaching credential at Harvard University, he lived in Israel and Belgium. Most importantly though, Roni has a huge heart and loves helping people.

To Get in Touch with Roni about Speaking at Your Organization, Scan This QR Code

Fun, useful, and transformative workshops and keynotes that lead to professional and personal development are Roni's trademark. Sessions are rooted in the fields of Emotional Intelligence, Positive Psychology, Mindfulness, Leadership Development, and Neuroscience.

Keynotes are designed to inspire your people, get them laughing, connected to each other, and reconnected to their purpose.

For educators, single- or multi-day workshops and retreats provide your staff with a deep dive into how to integrate positive psychology, mindfulness, and emotional intelligence strategies in their work with students and colleagues, as well as how to use these skills to increase their well-being in their daily life.

For leadership teams, onsite or offsite single- or multi-day workshops and retreats up-level the emotional resonance, coherence, trust, and creativity of your team. Your people will learn leadership and emotional intelligence skills experientially with one another and will reflect on and plan the integration of these skills into their daily work.

Workshop topics include:

- Joyful Leadership: Applying Positive Psychology, Emotional Intelligence, and Mindfulness to Your Life and Your Work
- You Can't Spell Equity without EQ: Applying Emotional Intelligence and Mindful Connections to allow Equity to Flourish
- The Power of Play and Connection!
- Relationships Above All
- Teaching to the Human Core
- Communicate Like a wizard!
- Dance with Your Gremlins!

Testimonials:

"Our district has had the opportunity to work with Roni Habib and EQ Schools over the past few years and the incredible value of this experience cannot be truly quantified. Roni helped guide our administrators and entire staff through one of the most challenging times in our district. The activities and encouragement he provided resulted in an increase in joy, gratitude, and appreciation despite the challenges we faced. We were able to retain our positive culture and even become stronger as a result. Roni and the EQ Schools' team made a difference in our district for our staff that absolutely trickled down to our students and entire community."

—Holly Edds, Superintendent of Orcutt Union School District

"Turlock Unified has had the honor and privilege of securing EQ Schools' Roni Habib to work with staff, parents, and community members over the last several years in our efforts to bring balance and insight during a difficult time for many. Roni's knowledge and personality brought immediate relief to those who were feeling anxiousness and trepidation about work-life obligations, parenting, and supporting scholars. Roni's work reinforced our administrators' work as well, providing a renewed sense of purpose and an 'I got this' mindset."

—Dana Tevenian, Superintendent, Turlock Unified School District

"Roni attended our staff retreat! At the end of the day, I had staff saying, 'There is no way you are going to top this one, he was great.' I truly agreed. Roni connected with my staff in such a personal way and brought staff together in ways they haven't been before. He made learning fun and showed us the importance of creating a similar environment for our students. His message—of being well connected and fully present in every moment—was powerful. My teachers are now using his strategies in the classrooms to better connect to their students, and they are seeing a difference in all grade levels."

—Cindy Gist, Principal and Superintendent of Sundale School

MORE FROM

Dave Burgess Consulting, Inc.

Since 2012, DBCI has published books that inspire and equip educators to be their best. For more information on our titles or to purchase bulk orders for your school, district, or book study, visit DaveBurgessConsulting.com/DBCIbooks.

More from the Like a PIRATE™ Series

Teach Like a PIRATE by Dave Burgess
eXPlore Like a PIRATE by Michael Matera
Learn Like a PIRATE by Paul Solarz
Plan Like a PIRATE by Dawn M. Harris
Play Like a PIRATE by Quinn Rollins
Run Like a PIRATE by Adam Welcome
Tech Like a PIRATE by Matt Miller

Lead Like a PIRATE™ Series

Lead Like a PIRATE by Shelley Burgess and Beth Houf
Balance Like a PIRATE by Jessica Cabeen, Jessica Johnson, and Sarah Johnson
Lead beyond Your Title by Nili Bartley
Lead with Appreciation by Amber Teamann and Melinda Miller
Lead with Collaboration by Allyson Apsey and Jessica Gomez
Lead with Culture by Jay Billy
Lead with Instructional Rounds by Vicki Wilson
Lead with Literacy by Mandy Ellis
She Leads by Dr. Rachael George and Majalise W. Tolan

Leadership & School Culture

Beyond the Surface of Restorative Practices by Marisol Rerucha

Change the Narrative by Henry J. Turner and Kathy Lopes

Choosing to See by Pamela Seda and Kyndall Brown

Culturize by Jimmy Casas

Discipline Win by Andy Jacks

Escaping the School Leader's Dunk Tank by Rebecca Coda and Rick Jetter

Fight Song by Kim Bearden

From Teacher to Leader by Starr Sackstein

If the Dance Floor Is Empty, Change the Song by Joe Clark

The Innovator's Mindset by George Couros

It's OK to Say "They" by Christy Whittlesey

Kids Deserve It! by Todd Nesloney and Adam Welcome

Leading the Whole Teacher by Allyson Apsey

Let Them Speak by Rebecca Coda and Rick Jetter

The Limitless School by Abe Hege and Adam Dovico

Live Your Excellence by Jimmy Casas

Next-Level Teaching by Jonathan Alsheimer

The Pepper Effect by Sean Gaillard

Principaled by Kate Barker, Kourtney Ferrua, and Rachael George

The Principled Principal by Jeffrey Zoul and Anthony McConnell

Relentless by Hamish Brewer

The Secret Solution by Todd Whitaker, Sam Miller, and Ryan Donlan

Start. Right. Now. by Todd Whitaker, Jeffrey Zoul, and Jimmy Casas

Stop. Right. Now. by Jimmy Casas and Jeffrey Zoul

Teachers Deserve It by Rae Hughart and Adam Welcome

Teach Your Class Off by CJ Reynolds

They Call Me "Mr. De" by Frank DeAngelis

Thrive through the Five by Jill M. Siler

Unmapped Potential by Julie Hasson and Missy Lennard

When Kids Lead by Todd Nesloney and Adam Dovico

Word Shift by Joy Kirr

Your School Rocks by Ryan McLane and Eric Lowe

Technology & Tools

50 Things to Go Further with Google Classroom by Alice Keeler and Libbi Miller

50 Things You Can Do with Google Classroom by Alice Keeler and Libbi Miller

140 Twitter Tips for Educators by Brad Currie, Billy Krakower, and
   Scott Rocco
Block Breaker by Brian Aspinall
Building Blocks for Tiny Techies by Jamila "Mia" Leonard
Code Breaker by Brian Aspinall
The Complete EdTech Coach by Katherine Goyette and Adam Juarez
Control Alt Achieve by Eric Curts
The Esports Education Playbook by Chris Aviles, Steve Isaacs, Christine
   Lion-Bailey, and Jesse Lubinsky
Google Apps for Littles by Christine Pinto and Alice Keeler
Master the Media by Julie Smith
Raising Digital Leaders by Jennifer Casa-Todd
Reality Bytes by Christine Lion-Bailey, Jesse Lubinsky, and Micah
   Shippee, PhD
Sail the 7 Cs with Microsoft Education by Becky Keene and
   Kathi Kersznowski
Shake Up Learning by Kasey Bell
Social LEADia by Jennifer Casa-Todd
Stepping Up to Google Classroom by Alice Keeler and Kimberly Mattina
Teaching Math with Google Apps by Alice Keeler and Diana Herrington
Teachingland by Amanda Fox and Mary Ellen Weeks
Teaching with Google Jamboard by Alice Keeler and Kimberly Mattina

Teaching Methods & Materials

All 4s and 5s by Andrew Sharos
Boredom Busters by Katie Powell
The Classroom Chef by John Stevens and Matt Vaudrey
The Collaborative Classroom by Trevor Muir
Copyrighteous by Diana Gill
CREATE by Bethany J. Petty
Deploying EduProtocols by Kim Voge, with Jon Corippo and
   Marlena Hebern
Ditch That Homework by Matt Miller and Alice Keeler
Ditch That Textbook by Matt Miller
Don't Ditch That Tech by Matt Miller, Nate Ridgway, and Angelia Ridgway
EDrenaline Rush by John Meehan
Educated by Design by Michael Cohen, The Tech Rabbi

The EduProtocol Field Guide by Marlena Hebern and Jon Corippo
The EduProtocol Field Guide: Book 2 by Marlena Hebern and Jon Corippo
The EduProtocol Field Guide: Math Edition by Lisa Nowakowski and
    Jeremiah Ruesch
The EduProtocol Field Guide: Social Studies Edition by Dr. Scott M. Petri
    and Adam Moler
Empowered to Choose: A Practical Guide to Personalized Learning by
    Andrew Easton
Expedition Science by Becky Schnekser
Frustration Busters by Katie Powell
Fully Engaged by Michael Matera and John Meehan
Game On? Brain On! by Lindsay Portnoy, PhD
Guided Math AMPED by Reagan Tunstall
Innovating Play by Jessica LaBar-Twomy and Christine Pinto
Instructional Coaching Connection by Nathan Lang-Raad
Instant Relevance by Denis Sheeran
Keeping the Wonder by Jenna Copper, Ashley Bible, Abby Gross, and
    Staci Lamb
LAUNCH by John Spencer and A.J. Juliani
Learning in the Zone by Dr. Sonny Magana
Lights, Cameras, TEACH! by Kevin J. Butler
Make Learning MAGICAL by Tisha Richmond
Pass the Baton by Kathryn Finch and Theresa Hoover
Project-Based Learning Anywhere by Lori Elliott
Pure Genius by Don Wettrick
The Revolution by Darren Ellwein and Derek McCoy
The Science Box by Kim Adsit and Adam Peterson
Shift This! by Joy Kirr
Skyrocket Your Teacher Coaching by Michael Cary Sonbert
Spark Learning by Ramsey Musallam
Sparks in the Dark by Travis Crowder and Todd Nesloney
Table Talk Math by John Stevens
Unpack Your Impact by Naomi O'Brien and LaNesha Tabb
The Wild Card by Hope and Wade King
Writefully Empowered by Jacob Chastain
The Writing on the Classroom Wall by Steve Wyborney
You Are Poetry by Mike Johnston
You'll Never Guess What I'm Thinking About by Naomi O'Brien

Inspiration, Professional Growth & Personal Development

Be REAL by Tara Martin

Be the One for Kids by Ryan Sheehy

The Coach ADVenture by Amy Illingworth

Creatively Productive by Lisa Johnson

Educational Eye Exam by Alicia Ray

The EduNinja Mindset by Jennifer Burdis

Empower Our Girls by Lynmara Colón and Adam Welcome

Finding Lifelines by Andrew Grieve and Andrew Sharos

The Four O'Clock Faculty by Rich Czyz

How Much Water Do We Have? by Pete and Kris Nunweiler

P Is for Pirate by Dave and Shelley Burgess

A Passion for Kindness by Tamara Letter

The Path to Serendipity by Allyson Apsey

Recipes for Resilience by Robert A. Martinez

Rogue Leader by Rich Czyz

Sanctuaries by Dan Tricarico

Saving Sycamore by Molly B. Hudgens

The Secret Sauce by Rich Czyz

Shattering the Perfect Teacher Myth by Aaron Hogan

Stories from Webb by Todd Nesloney

Talk to Me by Kim Bearden

Teach Better by Chad Ostrowski, Tiffany Ott, Rae Hughart, and Jeff Gargas

Teach Me, Teacher by Jacob Chastain

Teach, Play, Learn! by Adam Peterson

The Teachers of Oz by Herbie Raad and Nathan Lang-Raad

TeamMakers by Laura Robb and Evan Robb

Through the Lens of Serendipity by Allyson Apsey

The Zen Teacher by Dan Tricarico

Write Here and Now by Dan Tricarico

Children's Books

The Adventures of Little Mickey by Mickey Smith Jr.

Alpert by LaNesha Tabb

Alpert & Friends by LaNesha Tabb

Beyond Us by Aaron Polansky

Cannonball In by Tara Martin

Dolphins in Trees by Aaron Polansky

I Can Achieve Anything by MoNique Waters

I Want to Be a Lot by Ashley Savage

The Magic of Wonder by Jenna Copper, Ashley Bible, Abby Gross, and
   Staci Lamb

Micah's Big Question by Naomi O'Brien

The Princes of Serendip by Allyson Apsey

Ride with Emilio by Richard Nares

A Teacher's Top Secret Confidential by LaNesha Tabb

A Teacher's Top Secret: Mission Accomplished by LaNesha Tabb

The Wild Card Kids by Hope and Wade King

Zom-Be a Design Thinker by Amanda Fox

Made in the USA
Las Vegas, NV
20 May 2024

90174506R00134